AN AMPLE FIELD

I have, God knows, an ample field to plow
And feeble oxen.   —CHAUCER,
Canterbury Tales

An Ample Field

AMELIA H. MUNSON

1950

AMERICAN LIBRARY ASSOCIATION

CHICAGO

To all those
who have helped me learn
to read,—
a process still continuing

Foreword

THOSE WORKING in the field of young people's reading have long
wanted such a book as this hopes to be, something that will
provide orientation, bring together elusive ideas, vague thoughts,
unpublicized activities, and unformulated conclusions that may,
in the very setting down, show us how right we were all the
time in what we were doing and thinking, each one alone.

If this process of setting down means crystallization or such a
hardening of the mold that it shatters easily, it will be a per-
nicious book, to be banned at once. My hope is that it may
be an Aladdin's lamp and lose its dull and lifeless appearance
when the eager holder of it takes it into his own hands and
lets the warmth of his own personality bring it to a glow.

Names of books sprinkle the pages, for one is bound to go
from the general to the particular in discussing young people's
reading. No attempt has been made, however, to list all the
authors acceptable to young people or to set up a balanced
book collection. The books listed at the end of each chapter
are simply those mentioned during the discussion and should
lead to further exploration and discoveries on the part of
the reader.

Although it is the young people's librarians in the public
library who are directly addressed here, they are only the "front"

through whom I have sought to reach all those engaged in bringing together young people and books, including the large body of school librarians.

If any former students of mine at the Columbia University School of Library Service or colleagues in The New York Public Library should chance to read this book, they will find much here that is familiar to them. That cannot be avoided. What I have learned in my twenty-five years of library work, I have talked about as I have gone along. There are no new discoveries here.

> They would not find me changed from him they knew—
> Only more sure of all I thought was true.

Acknowledgments

I am grateful to the poets who have supplied me with just the right phrases for chapter headings and to the publishers who have granted me permission to quote them.

The heading for Chapter 4 is from Oliver Gogarty's "O Boys, O Boys!" in his *Selected Poems*, copyright 1933 by The Macmillan Company and used with their permission.

The heading for Chapter 6 is reprinted by permission of Harcourt, Brace and Company, Inc., from *Good Morning, America*, copyright, 1928, by Carl Sandburg.

The heading for Chapter 7 is from Robert Frost's "After Apple-Picking" and the lines at the end of the Foreword are from his "Into My Own," both of which are included in *Complete Poems of Robert Frost*, 1949, copyright 1916, 1930, 1950 by Henry Holt and Company, Inc., copyright 1944 by Robert Frost, and used by permission of the publishers.

The heading for Chapter 11 is from Archibald MacLeish's "Pony Rock," used by permission of the publishers, Houghton Mifflin Company.

The heading for Chapter 12 is from John Holmes's "After Two Years" in his *Address to the Living*, reprinted here by permission of Twayne Publishers, Inc.

And although no permission is required for this quotation,

it may be of interest to the reader to know that the heading for Chapter 1 is quoted from Henry Miller Lydenberg's *History of The New York Public Library,* 1922.

A special word of acknowledgment should go to the one responsible for my entry into the library profession and my activities therein—Mabel Williams, supervisor, counselor and friend.

Contents

PART ONE

CHALLENGE

☞   . . . they read excellent books, except the young
fry, who employ all the hours they are out of school
in reading the trashy, as Scott, Cooper, Dickens,
Punch, and the Illustrated News.

COGSWELL to TICKNOR
(Astor Library) 1854

CHAPTER 1

Youth

How WELL do you remember your teens? If you have been in
library work for any length of time, you may have learned anew
how priceless a thing is memory. No matter how complete the
bibliographic tools with which you are surrounded, there remain
many items of importance for which no indexes are provided,
and it devolves upon you to summon up from the vasty deeps
the recollection that will save the situation. You may as well
accept the fact that a trusting public, especially a youthful
public, believes that you have all the answers. You're a
librarian, aren't you? And somebody must have written something about this. What do you mean, you can't find it? And it
isn't just facts—it's people too, their faces, their names, their
troubles and joys that they've told you about. You don't mean
you've forgotten *them?* And the last book they read—you
helped them find it, remember? So ride your memory hard
and give it stuff to grow upon.

Now force it back a little, before library school, before college
days, before high school graduation. You won't need a psychi-
atrist's couch for this. Remember when you started to grow
up? And don't bother about telling me you weren't anything
like the boys and girls you see nowadays. Maybe you've forgotten something. Don't any books like *Seventeen* and *This*

*Let's start
with you*

Awful Age and *Seventeenth Summer* and *The Folded Leaf* awaken a rheumatic twinge or a rueful embarrassment? Some of these books are actually painful for an adult to read, so acute is his recollection, so vividly do they recreate his own past.

Of course there are excellent books on adolescent psychology to help you understand these young people with whom you hope to work, and I'll jot down the names of several good ones before I leave the subject. But it's silly to turn to them before getting all the answers you can from yourself. It means you're planning to approach these boys and girls as a librarian who knows his tools, not as a person with a living background. This is no explorer's trip you're taking; it's a journey through places where you once lived, and, if you will, you can add footnotes to any travel book about that territory; you can expand and dispute and document as you go along.

I can see one of those disputes hanging in the air right now. "I've done all this," you say impatiently, "and nothing in all my experience gives me any common ground of understanding with these young people of today." Well, I'm sorry. Perhaps there *is* too much difference between your youth and theirs, for social changes have come rapidly in this century, and one who does not move as the world moves feels lost indeed. Perhaps I sent you back to the wrong chronological age. Or perhaps you missed the run of children's diseases and will come down with a hard case later on, for it *is* hard, but glorious.

Adolescence   Do you remember the striking introduction Dickens wrote for his *Tale of Two Cities?* The beginning of it could be taken over intact as a description of adolescence:

It was the best of times, it was the worst of times, it was the age of wisdom, it was the age of foolishness, it was the epoch of belief, it was the epoch of incredulity, it was the season of Light, it was the season of Darkness, it was the spring of Hope, it was the winter of Despair, we had everything before us, we had nothing before us, we were all going direct to Heaven, we were all going direct the other way. . . .

We talk of youth as the hope of the world, but actually what do we let him do? Take over the city government for one day a year in Boys' and Girls' Week in some cities, vote at 18 in two states out of forty-eight, instigate and carry through some of his ideas for civic improvement in a few communities (as related in such books as Holbrook's *Children Object* and Hanna's *Youth Serves the Community*), but, for the most part, study, or, if he must leave school, work, and learn how things are done.

The newest phrase in education, however, as it is also one of the oldest ones (fathered by Aristotle) is "learn by doing." And as the elementary school sets up and studies a model community in its own classrooms, so must the high school age move out into the community and examine life at firsthand. They cannot hope to do this without the willing concurrence of their fellow citizens. Another highly respected educational term is "integration." And as the adolescent is unconsciously seeking a new and different integration with his family, so must he find one with the community. The library is one of the places where there should be no question about the recognition of his adult status.

Now it has always been my feeling that, whereas we insist upon and endeavor to instill in the young a respect for private property, we have never gone to sufficient pains with them to make clearly understood the whole province of public or common ownership. Until we do, we must accept mutilation and theft of public property as the inevitable concomitants of our lack of foresight. There is no blinking the difficulty of such teaching, for in our capitalistic society, the emphasis is still upon individual ownership—one of the acknowledged incentives. Democracy, too, puts the stress, and rightly, on the individual. But we are coming more and more to appreciate the impossibility of noncooperation in a shrinking world and to accept the idea that the individual is not entirely free to do whatever he likes even with his own possessions.

Public institutions

Young people can well understand common ownership. They are at the "gang" age and know that men must stand together and that they benefit by pooling not only their skills but their tools as well. The alert librarian will see to it that the young people in her community are given the concept of a public library that moved Benjamin Franklin to its establishment in our earliest days—that X hasn't money enough to buy all the books he needs, that Y hasn't room enough at home to keep piling up books, that Z is too busy with his own work to spend days hunting for certain answers that are to be found in books, and that if he and his neighbors could just get together and pool their resources, set up a place to keep all of the books that all of them may need (perhaps only once in a lifetime, but then, badly), and could hire someone to see to it that all the books are there and in good order and even to find the exact reference they sometimes want, and add books they haven't even heard of but will be glad to know about and will find useful, then everyone would benefit.

Young citizens   Let these boys and girls help establish book collections for their own age in this spirit. Let them work out a set of rules for their use, and, if these rules deviate decidedly from those now prevailing in your library, reexamine your procedures and see if they should be liberalized. In so far as possible, let the young people share in library tasks and routines. It may seem at times that you are doubling your own duties and troubles thereby, but you are building citizenship, and that is our function. Nowhere is there a better place to learn community interest, responsibility, and understanding than in the public or school library where there are no barriers of class, race, age, sex, religion, politics, or any other divisions that bedevil and beset the human race.

Function of the library   Perhaps you object to that statement, that building citizenship is our function. Battles have raged for years over the question: "What *is* the function of the public library?" And who am I to settle it? But if we pursue the question through easy stages—"to provide books"; *what books? for whom?*; "to make readers"; *what kind?*—shall we not arrive at the conclusion that, believing in the dignity and worth of every individual, we are seeking however indirectly to aid him in self-realization? And since we have no simple, unembarrassed way of saying that, we change it to "making good citizens." *Making superb persons* is what we really mean.

And those of us who are privileged to work with the formative period of adolescence have magnificent opportunities. Sometimes we are too close to the work to believe this and, anyway, much of our work has to be done on faith and the unseen results confidently believed in. Youth's period of impressionability may be as brief as a New York spring or a Los Angeles sunset, but let us go on believing it is there and see to it that the marks we put upon it shall be the kind we are glad to recognize as our own in later years.

Certain dominant characteristics of adolescence provide us with our opportunities. Each one has great potency. Each may develop beneficial or harmful influences. We shall need all our skill in dealing with them.

The adolescent— his traits

1. *Awareness of one's self*

This dawning realization of one's self as a peculiar individual, fascinating to explore and subject to no generalizations, opens up innumerable roads of influence. It usually makes boys and girls ready and eager for discussion, for argument even, for the gradual phrasing of their own philosophies, as they are forced into thought and contemplation. It can start them on a lifelong search for the real "I" that is the core of personality and for the best expression of that "I" and for something greater than one's self. It can keep them from developing into the crude and blatant and selfish person who is a perpetual adolescent. This is the beginning of a conscious formulation of personal philosophy and religion.

2. *Uncertainty*

Just because feelings are so strong and yet so fitful and because one is treated first as a child and then as an adult, the troubled adolescent veers sharply from one mood to another in his unconscious search for stability. This is a condition that encompasses us all at times in this seemingly unstable and irrational universe, and only by working together with patience will we find any solution. Don't think young people today are not uncertain; that cocksure manner of theirs is only an attempt at concealment of insecurity, but it is an easily pierced defense.

3. *Hero worship*

Does that sound old-fashioned? Still it is there to some extent. Newspapers make too much of hysterical bobby-soxers and of autograph-hounds of both sexes, but these manifestations are only symptoms of the urge for identification with the moment's favorite. The basic impulse is understandable—an escape from the desolation and the uncertainties of the self. The hero takes the place, too, of the family from which the adolescent is trying to break loose so as to establish a more mature relationship with them later on.

4. *Clannishness*

The desire to hunt in packs and again to seek anonymity in a desperate struggle away from the demands of the terrifying individual self is almost as difficult to reckon with as nationalism in our would-be One World. But there are seeds here for cooperative enterprise and joint action.

5. *Audacity of belief*

This is the age at which nothing is impossible. Mountains can be moved, and, if the oldsters do nothing about it, youth vows to do it himself. He feels infinite capacities within him and a long lifetime ahead. He is bound by nothing—not even prejudices.

To you— a word of advice   These, then, are the boys and girls with whom you are to work, whom you are to help to a realization of their highest selves. And before you roll up your sleeves and plunge in, with determination and perhaps some trepidation, may I give you a few words of advice as to your procedure?

1. Treat them as your contemporaries, as mature persons, but never forget that they have not yet attained that happy state and don't permit yourself to expect adult reactions.
2. Make yourself essential to them and then unnecessary. Win their confidence—merit it, rather—and then build up in each a deserved self-confidence and good, independent judgment.
3. Discover their individual interests and tastes and build upon them. Don't try to change them; keep searching for that real and highest "I" that may seem buried.

Of course there are a great many other pieces of advice that I long to give you, but these are the important ones, and you may notice that they all boil down to one thing: respect for the individual. Let young people be as different as may be; the greater the diversity we can welcome and deal with, the better for us and for them.

Are they all readers? Hardly. Some of them are, of course. *Young people* Some of them were once, in the halcyon days of childhood, *as readers* but have been distracted by too many other growing interests or have had their time too much taken over by other elements. Some of them find that, in comparison with radio, television, movies, or comics, reading calls for too much effort on their part. For a few, the very mechanics of reading set up an unscalable barrier so that they will never experience the pleasure and the diversion and the exceedingly great joy that can issue from a contact with books. Some may have been discouraged by having been given too advanced and esoteric materials, so that they are skeptical of finding anything at all of interest to themselves in print. Others read widely, unthinkingly, and indiscriminately. And some are natural and devoted readers whom nothing can alienate from their world of books. With all of these you must find common ground. You can do it only if you are interested in them as individuals.

What are their reading interests? That's an easy one to *Their reading* answer: simply a reflection of their other interests. Whatever *interests* they are really interested in they will read about if you can find the proper books. And what are they interested in? That's not so easy. In everything, I should say. Offhand (or even after painful reflection) I can't think of a single subject in which some young person isn't interested. But especially, let us say, in themselves and in the world around them, in the contemporary, "that which we have heard and seen, which our hands have handled"—in Life, really, and in all that adds to its beauty and its intelligibility. Isn't that enough to start with?

—and yours   You will find interests as diverse as pets, Plato, and plumbing; as fairy tales, fission, and football. Not in one person, of course, but somehow they'll have to unite in one person—YOU! How else can you even select books for them intelligently, to say nothing about introducing them to books and being ready to discuss anything with them at the drop of a hat? And if you think for a minute that baseball and the finer points of a vacuum tube and big game hunting and how to correct the drift of an airplane and the breakdown of a student nurse's job are irreconcilable elements, impossible to combine in one person's reading, you don't know the capacities of the human spirit. Some of these fields may be entirely foreign to you—"Yes, and" (I can hear you saying) "they can stay that way"—but aren't you forgetting why you're in this work? Your interest in the young people themselves will carry you over the difficulty of understanding or liking the subject matter, and you'll still be allowed some "blind spots" in your own reading. After all, you're not always going to be *talking* about books; another big part of your job is to *listen*. But young people do require active and intelligently interested listeners.

"Little man   You're appalled at all these requirements? How are you going
what now?"   to read all these books? Isn't there some short cut? I don't know of any. No list of books can do the work for you; no reviews I've ever seen are adequate. Worst of all, there's no special field of publishing for this great stretch of adolescent interests and abilities. Books have to be culled from both

adult and children's literature and tested for readability, entice-ability (to coin a word), and suitability. It's a continuous process, and the Devil take the hindmost.

Of course it's a job! What did you think? Maybe you're right. Maybe you ought to take up needlepoint instead.

HERE AND at the end of following chapters, books and aids are listed in accordance with their order of appearance in the text. Poems are noted as such.

Books mentioned in this chapter

TARKINGTON, BOOTH. Seventeen. Grosset
RYERSON, FLORENCE. This Awful Age. Appleton-Century
DALY, MAUREEN. Seventeenth Summer. Dodd, Mead
MAXWELL, WILLIAM. The Folded Leaf. Harper
DICKENS, CHARLES. A Tale of Two Cities. Dodd, Mead
HOLBROOK, SABRA. Children Object. Viking
HANNA, PAUL H. Youth Serves the Community. Appleton-Century

CROW, LESTER. Our Teen Age Boys and Girls. McGraw-Hill, 1945
HAVIGHURST, ROBERT J. and TABA, HILDA. Adolescent Character and Personality. Wiley, 1949
THOM, DOUGLAS A. Normal Youth and Its Everyday Problems. Appleton-Century, 1932
ZACHRY, CAROLINE B. Emotion and Conduct in Adolescence. Appleton-Century, 1940

A few good adolescent psychologies

Full of tumultuous life and great repose.
—PATMORE, *Magna Est Veritas*

CHAPTER 2

Books

IF WE WHO are attempting to attract young people to reading were asked to justify our endeavor, to explain just why we think it is worth while—"why should they read, anyhow?"—our glib, offhand answers might include these reasons: To gain perspective (history); to broaden their horizons (travel); to find their place in society (vocations); to acquire culture (arts); to understand the world about them (science, economics); to cultivate moral values (philosophy); to build up a body of information which will enable them to develop individual judgment.

Why read?

These are all admirable reasons, but, like some other admirable things, they seem a bit dull. The burden of self-improvement hangs heavily over them. If we turn for a moment from what we would prescribe for others, particularly for those younger than ourselves for whom we feel a certain responsibility, and examine our own voluntary reading, we shall discover an altogether different set of reasons.

First and foremost is *curiosity*, the desire to know at firsthand why everyone is reading a certain book, why everyone is talking about a certain author, what is going on in the world around us (certainly newspaper reading consumes an inordinate amount of our time), what lies back of some of the pressing questions of

Man is a curious animal

the day, how others have met the same problems that beset us. Books answer these questions, books and magazines and newspapers, and we turn to them naturally to satisfy that curiosity. And sometimes we may even have a desire to delve into the mechanics of writing, to learn how a certain writer gets his effects or why we are moved by a certain arrangement of letters on a page. This may lead into years of reading and study, but the basic urge remains curiosity. It accounts for by far the greatest portion of our reading, as I suppose it does for our acquisition of knowledge and for mental growth. Certainly it is a desirable trait and helps keep us young.

You may quarrel with my use of the term and insist that when you read many books along a certain subject or several books by the same author, you are reading because of interest rather than curiosity. I shall not contend the point. Perhaps curiosity is a broader term. Perhaps interest goes deeper. Which accounts for more of your reading? Be honest.

and a lazy one Then we read for pure *relaxation;* we turn to books as to a form of amusement or a sport. And although books may provide one with a form of solitaire, they are really at their best when they become the center of a social group.

This is a quiet, beautiful event,
  Four people reading poetry together,
Two men, two women, each in turn intent
  On one old volume bound in sober leather;
Fixed in one trance four minds all different,
  Like various landscapes in one lovely weather.

Not with stern drumbeats in one rhythm bound,
  On some incredible, brave march proceeding,
Nor in a dance, carefree, with scarves enwound,
  Could they seem closer, happier, more unheeding,
Than in the spell of this one poem's sound,
  Spoken by their four voices gravely reading.[1]

[1] From "Four People Reading" in *Blossoming Antlers* by Winifred Welles, copyright 1933. Used by permission of The Viking Press, Inc.

There was much lost as well as gained when oral reading went out of favor and silent reading received all the emphasis in schools. Reading aloud is an art that deserves revival. It is not to be undertaken casually, for it is merciless in its exposure of one's comprehension and appreciation of the passages read. But it is worth cultivating. It is a great amalgamating factor in a group of apparent dissidents. It provides a hard test, too, for a book to pass. Real values emerge, both in style and content, and make themselves felt and recognized. (The same is true for shoddiness.) Remember the injunction: "Read slowly. Read suspiciously. Read aloud." It is also a great asset in introducing books of high emotional appeal, for, with your eyes on your book and your voice under steady control, you can present material of such fineness and beauty to a group of boys or girls or both that they could not listen to it without self-consciousness, were your eyes free to scan their too expressive faces.

But I have digressed from the examination of our own voluntary reading in which I was considering its use for pure relaxation. This is where rereading comes in. We know what to expect from books that have never failed us; we can be confident and not at all fearful of disappointment. We can be certain, too, of refreshment and a harmonizing influence; why else would we turn to these books again? Some people would say that light reading belongs in this category (reading for relaxation)—"summer reading," light novels, romances, mysteries and adventure—and it is true that we usually approach this kind of reading with relaxed minds expecting that it will call for little mental effort. How rewarding it is as refreshment is another matter. The great books are, after all, the most refreshing, the greatest rebuilders of the spirit. It is too bad we can't learn this early in life, but no one can take another's word for it.

Again, we read because of *necessity*. There are times when *and is under* we seem to be literally driven into reading, when we must *pressures* somehow escape from a mood or find a way of creating a new one. Books give us that escape; books aid in that creation. They can accomplish the transformation in an incredibly short span of time, given some intelligent selection on our part. There are days, too, when our own mental dullness overwhelms us, when we need something on which to whet the mind. It may be the lowly detective story if actively read; it may be a book in a foreign language which goes so haltingly that we are infuriated into real effort; it may even be Euclid or Einstein where the utmost in concentration is demanded and time itself takes on new dimensions. Or we may be driven to find a companionship denied us in life, an answer to tormenting questions, a moral support for ideas mocked by our more cynical acquaintances. Books that we turn to at such times become the most cherished on our shelves, for into them we read part of ourselves. They have earned their place, and we refrain from dislodging them even when we no longer dare reread them. We need occasionally to remind ourselves that it is not only great literature that has healing qualities; inferior writing, unworthy writing, even, answers at times our momentary need and thereupon becomes endowed, for us, with qualities not actually inherent in either book or author. "So false it is that what we haven't, we can't give." And so there are literary skeletons in almost every reader's closet. We need not be ashamed of them; they emphasize the universality of human needs. If you have not had the shocking experience of finding in the most trivial reading matter a word or a phrase or more that has set you on the right path, then you probably have no respect for reading that is not literature. But the young people you work with are not so circumscribed, and you would do well to remember it and look beneath their enthusiasm for what seems to you second- or third-rate books for the real source of their satisfaction.

Curiosity—relaxation—necessity—these are the actual factors that influence us in our reading. Enjoyment? That is implied. Without it, all or any reading languishes. A fourth and final cause is *propinquity*—or proximity or availability or whatever you care to call it—the mere fact that the book is there, on the shelf, under your hand. It seems an obvious reason, and yet we all struggle against according it any great degree of influence in the whole pattern of our reading. I think it plays a very large part, and publishers who look for a great many distributing centers, friends who put books into our hands, librarians who leave books lying around the room in apparent carelessness are all wise as serpents. Cultivate the habit of dropping a book you would like to see read on a table in the midst of library traffic or put it on the truck with the books just returned. Everybody knows *those* are the good books!

Laziness again?

I have gone into the discussion of why we read, at some length, in order to show the difference between the causes that move us and the reasons we were giving for the reading of young people. Look at the latter again. Don't they seem a bit patronizing? A bit condescending? These boys and girls are not so different from ourselves. They are swayed by the same forces; they too are conscious of publicity and book fashions; they are driven by many of the same needs. Greater than all is the one encompassing phrase, "the pursuit of happiness." Reading for fun is the main thing; one sometimes wonders if reading without enjoyment accomplishes anything except the creation of distaste for the whole process.

Back to the young people

And we shall not be too insistent upon unanimity of response. Even in our zeal to make readers, we shall recognize that reading is only one of many sources of lifelong satisfaction. Each man is entitled to find his aesthetic expression in his own way. Our concern is that each of these young people shall find it somewhere.

☞ *Lauk a mercy on me, this is none of I.*
—Mother Goose

CHAPTER 3

You

LET'S START at the beginning. Let's assume that you are a librarian with training, employed in a public library where no special facilities exist for young people. There are plenty of young people in the community, however, and even in the library—too many of them, if you are to believe some of the adult borrowers who find them noisy, inconsiderate, and ubiquitous. You're rather sympathetic with them, yourself, and the librarian-in-charge, noting it and seizing an opportunity, asks you to initiate a program to deal with the situation. *Let's suppose*

What do you do?

First. Examine your philosophy of librarianship. Know why you want to attract young people to books. This goes deeper than merely building up the use of the library and adding to the circulation and registration figures. It digs right down into your genuine belief in the power of books and what they can do for the individual, into the need that every human being has not only to keep abreast of the thought of today but to be aware of the great thoughts of the past that constitute our heritage. If this belief in the power of the recorded word, the value of communication, and the impact of great ideas is strong within you, is indeed basic to your professional thinking, then you can face your opportunity with understanding and zest. *Start here*

Without it, whatever success you may have will be spurious. This does not mean that you will always be going around talking about the great influence and worth of books. Your belief may never be stated in words, but it must be there as a faith to sustain you in a field of work where measurement of results is almost impossible to secure.

??????   *Second.* Look around you at the young people already in your library and at those others in the community whom you never see. Ask yourself questions about them: Why do they come? What books do they ask for? Is your library used only as a reference room for school assignments? Is it a dating center? Are any of these young people out of school? Working? What about the ones you never see? What kinds of homes are represented in the community? Churches? Schools? Recreation centers? Are there any youth-serving organizations in your community? If so, what are their programs? Whom do they attract? How complete is their coverage? What reputation do the young people generally have? Is there much juvenile delinquency? Are the adults concerned? Where does the library best fit into the community pattern? When you have answered these questions as best you can, talk with some of your young people and get their ideas and suggestions.

A room of one's own   *Third.* Presumably they will want a *locus* as well as a *modus operandi*, and, although libraries differ greatly in the amount of space they can afford for this work, there must be some center—a room, if possible; if not, an alcove or even a section of shelving. Select the place, then, and let your young people help you in setting it up, making it attractive, choosing the books, and giving it publicity.

Not— "Me, too!"   *Fourth.* Now you can branch out. Now you can go to these other organizations with something of your own to offer and invite their inspection. But if you solicit their aid earlier than this, you run the risk of becoming supplementary rather than complementary to them. All agencies should work together on a basis of equality.

Fifth. From the young people attracted to your center or from the schools or from out-of-school groups, form a Youth Council or Advisory Board or Young People's Committee, a loosely organized but well-selected unit to help in developing ideas. "Programs" may be too ambitious a word, but some programs are bound to be suggested, for young people want to talk together and exchange ideas. There should be a way of satisfying this natural desire. Once the library realizes its importance and feels some compulsion to meet it, a way will be found.

Let youth help!

All of this assumes that you are not only asked to submit a plan for this work, but that you are given time and scope to develop it. It assumes further that you are a person who understands young people and respects them, who knows at firsthand the books they read and can be induced to read, who knows how and when to talk and how and when to listen, and who can deal persuasively not only with young people but with the other members of the library staff upon whom much of the success or failure of any special work will necessarily depend. You need not be an expert in public relations to realize how quickly and completely the friendliness and confidence you have seen built up toward your institution can be shattered by one unthinking person's impatience or discourtesy.

The job grows

If you have had no special training for work with young people, you will probably be reaching out for something in print that you can rely on to support your findings and suggest procedures. Two publications in particular will offer guidance: *The Public Library Plans for the Teen Age* and *A Youth Library in Every Community.* The first publication outlines the work and sets standards for it in administration, personnel, book collection and services, and space and equipment. (This may be just the thing you need to bring to the attention of your librarian.) It also contains, in the appendix, excerpts from leading articles on work with young people that have appeared in professional journals in recent years, and the lively comments

Help is at hand

it has exhumed will bolster your spirit and increase your determination. The other brochure will provide you with graphic
representation of young people's work as it is being conducted
all over the country.

Both of these are descriptive of public libraries, but don't
stop with them. Familiarize yourself with present-day trends in
school libraries, especially as presented in that exciting chapter,
"The Library a Reading Center," in Lucile Fargo's *The Library
in the School.*

Book lists   If you want book lists, there are excellent ones, chief among
them three well-known ones: *By Way of Introduction,* an
attractive, well-annotated list in which over a thousand books
for the high school age are grouped by reading interests under
21 headings; *Books for You,* a list of about two thousand titles
for the four years of high school "arranged by themes and types"
in 11 large groupings; and *Books for Young People,* an unan-
notated but annually revised list of about fourteen hundred
books for young people between the ages of 13 and 18, also
arranged according to subject interest.

Such lists may serve to buttress your own choices or suggest
unconsidered interests or startle you into questioning, but
remember that, even in the matter of book selection, *no list
can do the work for you.* It will be your own acquaintance with
books that will be called into play and your own judgment that
must finally sustain you.

Reviews and listings of current books selected for young
people may be found in *The Booklist* and in the *Library Journal.*
You would do well, also, to watch the section, "Outlook Tower,"
in *The Horn Book* and keep in touch with your colleagues
through *Top of the News.* And I don't see how you can keep
house without May Lamberton Becker's book for the teens,
Adventures in Reading, as good today as it was twenty years ago.
A new edition was issued in 1946, bringing the book lists up to
date but requiring very little revision otherwise. It's sprightly
and stimulating (and restful at the same time) and highly

informative, and, even if you don't need it, it's like money in the bank to have it around.

These aids are for your own guidance and reassurance when the occasion comes, as come it will, when you feel yourself utterly incapable of coping with the task you have undertaken. You will not need them for challenge or stimulus: these will come from the young people themselves, even though they may never approach you directly with requests for your assistance.

They may give the impression of complete self-sufficiency as they roam through the library, irked by restraints and sure of their own decisions, but you may confidently tell yourself that down underneath there is a desire for occasional advice and for reading guidance—vigilant, sympathetic, unobtrusive. Young people want it, as they want stability. Not that they will ask for it, but they like to know it is there. They will frequently spurn a consciously directed form of assistance; they will scorn anyone whom they suspect of trying to improve their taste; and while they recognize and welcome sincerity on the part of an older person, they will run away from earnestness. It is too obviously loaded.

S O S

Reading guidance is a term capable of many interpretations and many abuses. It may be simply stated as book selection; it may sound as complex as bibliotherapy. It is not the hanging-over-one's-shoulder-and-breathing-down-one's-neck form of supervision. It is not censorship. It is not the imposition of a librarian's personal taste in books or of her own sense of values, however fine. It is an intelligent evocation of the reader's highest powers, a stimulant and a continued nourishment to the growth of his independent judgment. And the concern of the librarian must always be, not for agreement, but for the consistent development of the individual. All of us, fundamentally, aspire to The Good, The True, and The Beautiful, but there are diverse ways of reaching it: there is the artist's way, the scientist's, the saint's, the mechanic's, the business man's, the politician's,—yes, and the dawdler's, the idler's, the ragman's, bagman's. . . .

Reading guidance

And we are here to clear whatever obstacles we can from the path of the ascent.

Book
selection
The best definition of book selection I have heard runs like this: "the practice of supplying people with the books they want, and of setting before them the books they don't know that they want."[1] Guidance enters into both parts of that picture, but the fun of it is in the latter half. We usually think of books as answering any of three demands: information, recreation, and inspiration. Or, considering the needs of the individual reader, we may be aware of his occupational needs (professional, technical and economic books), his social needs (social science, history, best sellers, psychology), and his inner needs (whatever ministers to the spirit). These last books are the ones he seldom asks for but is deeply pleased to find, and they should be at his hand. All this is true for adolescents and adults alike.

Who's to be
served?
Let us examine that definition more closely—"to supply people with the books they want." Is that really the public library's function? Controversy over this point will probably never cease in professional circles, and it may be unwise to inject the argument here. But the big question remains: Is it to be a *public* library? And the inescapable fact is that, as a library selects its books, it determines its readers. There should be on its shelves books suitable for and acceptable to all its potential readers.

That does not mean (to return to the adolescent patiently awaiting our consideration) that *all* the "series" books, *all* the "rags-to-riches" books, *all* the "bait" books should be provided, but neither should they be excluded *in toto*. Taste is a peculiar thing, impossible to define and so integrated a part of the personality that one defends it unconsciously. It is not for the librarian to condemn the reading taste of an individual or a community and refuse to cater to it, unless it borders on the vicious and the obscene, but rather so to present books of un-

[1] From a lecture by Eliza Marquess, The New York Public Library.

questioned superiority as to give their graces full play and let their merits prevail. To set beside the shallow, the transluscent; beside the extravagant, the satisfying; beside the sensational, the desperate realities; to confront falsity with sincerity and disbelief with hope is to establish such grounds for the growth of a sense of true values that taste itself, that sensitized response of the individual, will change as it must to meet it.

But this action properly belongs to the second half: "to set before them the books they don't know that they want." Therein lies the great enjoyment and reward and opportunity for leadership for the library profession. We are the Calebs and Joshuas who have been sent on ahead to find the land flowing with milk and honey and we can come back to report, bearing fruit and grain undreamed of. True, we have exercised some discrimination in what we have brought, but the land from which it was taken is rich and pleasant beyond our telling.

"To set before them" may mean no more than its literal expression. With some readers, that will suffice. But the term may be expanded to include every device by which a natural scoffer or an indifferent or callous onlooker may be brought to participate in the enjoyment of books: displays, exhibits, readings, book talks, book reviews, film forums, discussion groups, dramatics, quiz shows, broadcasting, storytelling, book games, impersonations, special collections, clubrooms, lounges, bookbinding, illustration, printing, recordings . . . , promotional devices, to be sure, but each with its special use, each serving a special group, and each brought into play only when indicated as particularly helpful. For each device the librarian should have full understanding of its use, intuition as to the occasion for it, and the ability and equipment to set it in motion.

But first, the books themselves.

AMERICAN LIBRARY ASSOCIATION. DIVISION OF LIBRARIES FOR CHILDREN AND YOUNG PEOPLE, AND ITS SECTION, THE YOUNG PEOPLE'S READING ROUND TABLE. COMMITTEE ON POST-WAR   *Aids noted in this chapter*

PLANNING. The Public Library Plans for the Teen Age. A.L.A., 50 East Huron St., Chicago 11. 1948

AMERICAN LIBRARY ASSOCIATION. YOUNG PEOPLE'S READING ROUND TABLE. A Youth Library in Every Community. The Sturgis Printing Company, Sturgis, Michigan. 1948

FARGO, LUCILE. The Library in the School. A.L.A., 50 East Huron St., Chicago 11. 1947

AMERICAN LIBRARY ASSOCIATION, NATIONAL EDUCATION ASSOCIATION, and NATIONAL COUNCIL OF TEACHERS OF ENGLISH. JOINT COMMITTEE. By Way of Introduction. 2d ed. A.L.A., 50 East Huron St., Chicago 11. 1947

NATIONAL COUNCIL OF TEACHERS OF ENGLISH. Books for You. The Council, 211 West 68th St., Chicago 21. 1945

BOOKS FOR YOUNG PEOPLE, prepared by the Young People's Librarians, The New York Public Library, and issued annually as the January number of Branch Library Book News. The New York Public Library, 476 Fifth Ave., New York 18

THE BOOKLIST, published semimonthly, September through July, and monthly in August. American Library Association, 50 East Huron St., Chicago 11

LIBRARY JOURNAL, published semimonthly from September through June, monthly in July and August. R. R. Bowker Company, 62 West 45th St., New York 19

THE HORN BOOK MAGAZINE, published bimonthly. The Horn Book Inc., 248 Boylston St., Boston 16

TOP OF THE NEWS, published four times a year by the American Library Association, Division of Libraries for Children and Young People, and mailed free to the membership. The Sturgis Printing Company, Sturgis, Michigan.

BECKER, MAY LAMBERTON. Adventures in Reading. New ed. Lippincott, 1946

PART TWO

RESOURCES

☞ *O Boys, the things I've seen!*
The things I've done and known!
If you knew where I have been . . .
You never would leave me alone.
　　　　　—GOGARTY, *O Boys, O Boys!*

CHAPTER 4

Books
of Adventure

WHAT BOOKS for young people? Where are you to start? How do you assemble a collection for your newly set-aside shelves? There are no publishers' catalogs to answer this question, although interest in teen agers is strong and some fumbling attempts are being made. There are helpful book lists, as the preceding chapter indicates, and the best of them are made by *persons like yourself* who are in direct touch with young people and can reflect and interpret their enthusiasms. After all, you must be able to do some independent thinking in this matter— read, consider, reject, experiment, accept, promote. Librarians become adept at fitting the book to the borrower as they read; it is a professional accomplishment that grows with indulgence and can seldom be altogether shaken off and completely dissociated even from one's personal reading. You learn also to let books group themselves together as you read—a phrase, a character, a locale, a denouement, a style of writing, anything that will serve to set up echoes of other reading and bring books into one company. Comparisons, contrasts, parallels, even plagiarisms are noted as prime factors in forming judgment. So let's start, again not with book lists and reviews, but with your own young people and yourself.

I hope you have a good background of reading in both adult

What books?

and children's literature, for all of this will be useful. And I hope you have some marked enthusiasms of your own that you will not be too reticent about sharing. Even though your reading preferences are not to be imposed upon young people, they are not to be entirely effaced. Special delights are needed in this work; they help spread the contagious idea that there is fun to be found in reading, and it is the tangential point where the line of your mature interest strikes the arc of young people's reading that will make the sparks fly.

Adventure   Ask some of these boys what kind of reading they want, and almost the first answer will be "a good story." That means *adventure*. It usually means a plot, complete with hero and villain (heroine accepted but not essential), rapid narration unimpeded by description or documentation (in the case of historical novels), plenty of conversation, and a sound conclusion. This is almost a description of a good "boy's book," ages 10-12, but it is also all that a good many adults demand from a book. At least it is a point of departure. So long as the element of adventure is present, almost any country, any period, any subject matter, any element—sea, earth, or air—may be introduced. Mysteries are liked. Fantastic tales, especially scientific ones, are welcome. Nor is there any sharp line drawn here between fiction and nonfiction: biographies and books of travel that contain these qualities are as readily devoured (the life of Houdini, the experiences of Ditmars, the travels of Halliburton). One fact militates against autobiographies or any books written in the first person, the loss of a certain amount of suspense, since "I" undoubtedly lived to see the story ended. (There have, of course, been a few notable exceptions.) This antipathy to "I" books is felt strongest when one is leafing through a book preparatory to reading. A hint or two about some hazardous point of the narrative will usually suffice to overcome the initial distrust. Indeed some boys will scarcely believe, when you remind them of it, that certain books they have thoroughly enjoyed are actually of this kind.

The range of "adventure stories" may seem to the adult unlimited, since every human story is an adventure, but the youthful reader is more demanding. He does not insist that the author write at the top of his lungs as did Halliburton, or stretch the truth, like the Baron, or hurtle from one highly perilous spot to another in the style of the gusty Three Musketeers. But there should at least be peril in the narrative and need for hasty action, even if it is only the standing of a baseball club that is at stake.

Sports stories are always in favor, with baseball at the top but football, hockey, and track finding their followers also. And don't think for a moment that a love story at the college level, with a rousing football game thrown in, constitutes what your teen ager calls a sports story. The game's the thing. The characters must be believable, the game hotly contested, the phraseology contemporary, and the more technical expressions the better. This last requirement seems to pertain to all books for boys: the more technical knowledge they find scattered around through their reading, the more their appetites grow. But John Tunis has proved that a so-called sports story can carry its weight of social significance and still be popular: the theme of racial discrimination in *All American*, of good government in *A City for Lincoln*, and of clean sportsmanship in *The Keystone Kids*.

The appeal of sport is wide enough to include: biographies of outstanding figures—Bob Feller, Lou Gehrig, Sonje Henie, Walter Johnson, Jackie Robinson, Knute Rockne, Babe Ruth; histories of big league teams—the Dodgers, the Pirates, the Red Sox, the Yankees; accounts of famous contests; illustrated and factual presentations of play and players which are a delight to pore over and may be used to lead into other books—*The Story of Baseball in Words and Pictures* by John Durant, *How to Box* by Joe Louis, *The Story of Basketball* by Lamont Buchanan; and finally the technical books that explain the sport, give advice on improving one's game, and include all the latest rules and the highly relished details.

Sports

School stories

For teen-age boys, sports books undoubtedly lead the field in interest and should be first purchase for your shelves. They have largely taken over the place formerly occupied by school stories and in many instances touch upon school life as well—a fascinating subject for both boys and girls, reflecting, as it does, the contemporary world they know so well. John Tunis' books, for example, deal with the amateur rather than the professional in sport and with the high school age and surroundings. Almost the only school stories for boys that have survived the ruthless winnowing of the years are the Lawrenceville tales of Owen Johnson, and even they are beginning to seem a bit historical (a kinder word than 'dated'). Girls have fared better, and every year seems to bring out its plethora of school and college stories from which one must sort out the few that have genuine characterization and vitality.

Another caution for you

This may be as good a time as any to warn against a static collection. However wisely your books may be chosen when your young people's room or alcove is first established, however much in favor the books seem to be, the collection will soon lose its attraction if frequent changes in book stock are not made, if new titles and new editions are not constantly appearing and outmoded ones disappearing, or if several duplicates of a book, no matter how popular, appear on the shelves at the same time. It is wise to have enough duplicates to satisfy demand (is it ever possible?), but it detracts from the appeal of the book if they are all visible.

Interest in sports springs from love of the contest and may be utilized to introduce many different kinds of reading matter. Opdyke, in a book on methods of teaching English, has said that it is possible to start with a poem like "Casey at the Bat" and, by going through a series of poems based on rivalry, come out with "Pheidippides."[1] The statement is both true and challenging and indicates the kind of book association by which you will be continually obsessed.

[1] John Opdyke, *In the Service of Youth* (Pitman, 1928).

The story of "Twister" McCoy, in *Mr. Mergenthwirker's Lobblies,* who upset baseball games by his ability to pitch balls into the fourth dimension is a teaser for the sports fan and lands him unexpectedly in the field of fantasy where, he would have said, he is less at home. But here again adventure is in plenteous store and heroic characters emerge. *Fantasy*

The native American propensity for tall tales and the ability to improvise gain ready acceptance for Paul Bunyan, Pecos Bill, Tony Beaver, John Henry, Joe Magarac, and other big-time leaders in American folklore. There are various retellings of these yarns; for your young people's collection, choose the more adult ones. The whole trend of the collection, incidentally, should be toward adult writing, though many of the simpler books are needed for boys and girls who have reading difficulties or who find it impossible to leap with one bound from the reading of stories to novels. *Tall tales*

'Fantasy' is probably a term your down-to-earth teen ager will sniff at and couple with fairy tales which have been completely outgrown. Decked out as "science fiction" or "scientific tales" instead of "fantasy," these books at once attract followers. The school of writing started by Jules Verne and H. G. Wells has grown to such mammoth proportions that librarians must be critical in their selection. The main thing is to be sure that the tales include enough reality to keep the imagination from bogging down and that the writer does not go contrary to known scientific data. *Science fiction*

Of particular interest are books on interplanetary travel which, to some untutored minds, are no more fantastic or unreal than many of the technical books on rockets, jet propulsion, and superstratosphere flying. These the teen ager takes in his stride.

Flying is now such a casual part of our daily life that books dealing with the subject no longer have the fascination that attached to them before the Second World War. Yet it is by no means a subject to be disregarded. Like the sports enthusiast, the reader of aviation books wants all kinds of material: not only *Aviation* stories but firsthand adventures in the air (not necessarily connected with fighting), pictorial and technical books, up-to-the-minute developments in the field, and vocational information. It does not distress him to find that certain fliers write with distinction, notably Saint-Exupéry and Anne Lindbergh, or that a trained aeronautical engineer like Nevil Shute can turn his hand to excellent story writing, or that a combat fighter, intent on his job, can still embody his feelings succinctly and movingly in a sonnet, as did Pilot Officer John G. Magee, Jr. Like most of his contemporaries, he reads for content with no conscious thought of style, and yet fine writing, nervous, sinewy, functional writing that never obtrudes but somehow satisfies by its very presence, will come eventually to make its mark, so that lack of it will be noticeable and irritating. That, of course, is what we hope for and why we select books with such care, even in overgrown fields like "mysteries," "westerns," etc.

Mysteries and westerns, by the way, are two very popular areas of reading both for adolescents and adults, and so strenuously do writers labor to meet the market demand that considerable discrimination must be exercised in book purchasing, else will the lean kine eat up all the fat ones. Interest in cowboys and in crime is genuine and natural and should be recognized and respected. The reader is entitled to good books in each category rather than run-of-the-mill ones and should be enabled to develop some grounds for comparison and judgment.

Detective stories   One can hardly think of mysteries or detective stories without reference to the great man by whom all detectives are bound to be measured, Sherlock Holmes himself. His adventures should be among the first to be read so that some standard of comparison may be set up; then the Father Browns, the Charlie Chans, the Hercule Poirots, the Reggie Fortunes, the Nero Wolfes, the Dr. Thorndykes, the Lord Peter Wimseys, the Mr. Pinkertons, the Miss Silvers, and the Miss Witherses take their place, and each is found to have stature. Acquaintance with the doings of these agents and with the well-knit plots of their authors and with such other and older favorites as Wilkie Collins' *Moonstone*, Poe's *Murders in the Rue Morgue*, A. E. W. Mason's *At the Villa Rose*, Mary Roberts Rinehart's *Circular Staircase*, and Anna Katharine Green's *Leavenworth Case* leaves the reader rather stern in his demands upon the writers of detective fiction and far less easily satisfied than he would otherwise be.

Here, too, one notes in working with young people their readiness to forget the line we draw between fiction and non-fiction and to reach out for books on the F.B.I., on the workings of the police force, and the Special Intelligence. It would be heartening to be able to record an accompanying interest in law, but, except for the popularity of the Perry Mason and the Ephraim Tutt stories, there is little or no evidence to be had.

And yet young people instinctively side with the law in their reading and discussion of crime and of social problems. Not that they are uncritical or that they consider laws to be sacrosanct and established beyond possibility of change or modification, but they do seem to be aware of the necessity for some organized authority in any community. Many of the books they read on the '49ers and the rise of the Vigilantes develop this idea logically and unobtrusively.

Westerns have had neither the outstanding figures nor authors that have added luster to the detective story field, yet it is possible even here to highlight a few. Owen Wister's *The Virginian* is probably the best known "quality" western. The stories of Eugene M. Rhodes provide authentic background and local color for succeeding writers to gain by. Will James has vividly presented the cowboy complete with lingo in fiction, autobiography and lively sketches. Among the most dependable writers of our day are Peter Field, Evan Evans, Dane Coolidge, and William M. Raine.

Interest in westerns may be played upon to introduce the Lomax collection of ballads, Larkin's *Singing Cowboy*, such an anthology as Ruth Barnes's *I Hear America Singing*, with its

Westerns

representative ballads selected by the young people themselves, or scattered poems like William Rose Benét's "The Horse Thief" or Conrad Aiken's "The Kid."

Certain biographies can easily be introduced here: Buffalo Bill, Kit Carson, Davy Crockett, Long Lance, Sitting Bull, Daniel Boone, and historical narrative dealing with westward expansion, though I would hesitate to recommend Parkman's *Oregon Trail* to a boy who had just completed *Powder Valley Showdown* and wanted another book "just like it." After all, we have to use a little sense in these matters and sometimes play a waiting game.

To many adults, westerns are the present-day successors to the old "dime novel" and only a notch above "the pulps." But if you condemn such reading—*any* reading, for that matter— you will only drive its followers into rebellious continuance and zealous defense of it and to a lack of faith in your judgment. Accept their interest as a natural outgrowth of the early "cops and robbers" game, and remember, as Irvin Cobb recommends, that "if this country had not had a pioneer breed of Buckskin Sams and Deadwood Dicks, we should have had no native school of dime novelists."[2]

It is true, as with mysteries, that the demand for westerns is large and steady and that, in such mass production, values are slight if not entirely lacking. Science fiction now seems threatened by similar impairment. But the thing for us to remember is that such reading is not harmful unless it destroys the taste for and interest in any other kind. It may well mark a phase in the individual's development, on a par with series books—the old, old search for Superman. Once we recognize it as such, we can be generous in dealing with it. The words of Chesterton, explaining the peculiar fascination of Dickens's characters ("Dickens did not strictly make a literature; he made a mythology"), may well be studied, as he goes on to examine the common hunger of mankind:

[2] Irvin S. Cobb, *A Plea for Old Cap Collier* (Doubleday, 1921), p. 54.

Herein lies the peculiar significance, the peculiar sacredness even, of penny dreadfuls and the common printed matter made for our errand-boys. Here, in dim and desperate forms, under the ban of our base culture, stormed at by silly magistrates, sneered at by silly schoolmasters,—here is the unmistakable voluminousness, the thousand and one tales of Dick Deadshot, like the thousand and one tales of Robin Hood. Here is the splendid and static boy, the boy who remains a boy through a thousand volumes and a thousand years. Here in mean alleys and dim shops, shadowed and shamed by the police, mankind is still driving its dark trade in heroes.[3]

Of course the search for a hero is one thing; for the "man on horseback," quite another. Your teen agers would be as appalled as you if they suspected themselves of wanting dictatorial solutions for the world's problems.

Guidance again

After all, the only way to combat devotion to cheap and meretricious writing is by developing a taste for books of genuine worth that, at the same time, fulfil the reader's requirements for perilous situations and the resourcefulness to meet them. Jim Hawkins, hiding in the apple barrel, holding his breath to listen to Silver's plans and realizing that "the lives of all the honest men aboard depended on me alone"; the low, unexpected but providentially near voice of Alan Breck calling to David, "Jouk in here among the trees," just as encirclement seemed certain; the Scarlet Pimpernel running his wild and unending risks; Mr. Pickwick gallantly leaping into every breach that offered; Major Joppolo tossing away his career rather than disappoint the people of Adano who wanted and needed their bell—these can offer sturdy competition even to two-gun men.

Sea stories

As for those who sail the seas, there can be no question of their capacity. Even in our day of motor driven ships, the sea remains an unruly element, baffling and thwarting those who would tame her. There is not only adventure but romance and a touch of mystery in the tales of old sailormen and voyagers.

[3] Reprinted by permission of Dodd, Mead & Company from *Charles Dickens* by G. K. Chesterton, copyright 1906, 1934 by G. K. Chesterton.

From the simple clarity of Howard Pease to the psychological involvements of Conrad, from the bluster of Sabatini to the restraint of Alan Villiers, from the vivid reality of Masefield's "Dauber" to the "wine-dark sea" of Homer, there is magic for all who read.

Adventure adds a gleam to daily living. Older readers turn to such books for a splendor that has been lacking in their lives, but youth employs them as guidebooks for life that is to come. Perhaps not in the high places nor on lonely seas nor in crowded thoroughfares, but somewhere, sometime, the moment will come that calls for all his valor, all his resources. For that moment he trains.

> We were not meant for pinched things, to be poor,
> But still we scrape life bare of large or deep,
> As housewives scrape their crocks. Thus stay we small;
> Thus scarcity for scarcity is sure.
> Oh we must loose ourselves from what we keep,
> Begin with splendor then, or not at all![4]

As youth reads and grows and grows and reads, he becomes interested in what other men have actually done, not dreamed of doing, in moments of desperation or opportunity. His heroes need not all be fictional.

Personal history   He can respond to the self-sacrifice of Oates, walking out of Captain Scott's tent in the Antarctic, to a storm he knew he could not survive, hoping thereby to free his companions from a delay that meant certain death; he can return with Father Damien to an existence bitterly removed from living; he can rise to the occasion with Walter Scott, faced with a bankruptcy that involved others innocent as himself, and struggle for years to wring from his writing money enough to save them from any deprivation; he can risk his life with Tom Eadie to rescue a

---

[4] From "Dearth" in *White April and Other Poems*, copyright 1930 by Lizette Woodworth Reese. Reprinted by permission of Rinehart & Company, Inc., publishers.

BOOKS OF ADVENTURE 39

fellow diver; he can sense the drama in Walter Reed's fight against yellow fever, even if he were not reading it in the play form of *Yellow Jack*, and count O'Hara and Lazear among his heroes; he can understand and be grateful for the sport-writer's verdict on Lou Gehrig: "the gamest guy I ever saw." Deep within him is this urge toward identifying himself with characters of daring and of nobility—as Tarkington understood when he had Willie Baxter cast himself in the role of Sydney Carton— and biographies that vividly present all-too-human men who, at the compelling moment, rose to their full stature will be grist to his mill.

Wherever dangers beckon, there will always be youth to follow though he cannot explain why he goes. Margaret Scoggin gave due recognition to that fact when she entitled her anthology of true adventures *The Lure of Danger*. Meserve, the preacher in Robert Frost's poem "Snow," probably expressed it as well as anyone could. All but blocked in his homeward journey by a heavy snowstorm which his horses could hardly plough through, *"The lure of danger"*

> "Three hours to do four miles—a mile an hour,
> Or not much better. Why, it doesn't seem
> A man could move that slow and move,"

he stops for a short respite at the Coles's house. When he indicates his readiness to resume his journey, Mrs. Cole cannot understand him:

> "But why, when no one wants you to go on?
> Your wife—she doesn't want you to. We don't,
> And you yourself don't want to. Who else is there?"

Says Meserve,

> "Save us from being cornered by a woman.
> Well, there's"—She told Fred afterward that in
> The pause right there, she thought the dreaded word
> Was coming, 'God.' But no, he only said,
> "Well, there's—the storm. That says I must go on.

That wants me as a war might if it came.
Ask any man."[5]

KELLOCK, HAROLD. Houdini. Blue Ribbon

DITMARS, RAYMOND L. Thrills of a Naturalist's Quest. Macmillan

HALLIBURTON, RICHARD. Seven League Boots. Garden City

RASPE, RUDOLPH. The Surprising Adventures of Baron Munchausen. Hale, Cushman

DUMAS, ALEXANDRE. The Three Musketeers. Dodd, Mead

TUNIS, JOHN. All American. Harcourt, Brace
————— A City for Lincoln. Harcourt, Brace
————— The Keystone Kids. Harcourt, Brace

FELLER, BOB. Strikeout Story. Barnes

GRAHAM, FRANK. Lou Gehrig, a Quiet Hero. Putnam

HENIE, SONJE. Wings on My Feet. Prentice-Hall

TREAT, ROGER L. Walter Johnson. Messner

ROBINSON, JACKIE. My Own Story. Greenberg

LOVELACE, DELOS. Rockne of Notre Dame. Putnam

WELDON, MARTIN. Babe Ruth. Crowell

DURANT, JOHN. The Dodgers. Hastings House

LIEB, FREDERIC. The Pittsburgh Pirates. Putnam

HIRSHBERG, ALBERT. The Red Sox, the Bean, and the Cod. Waverly House

GRAHAM, FRANK. The Yankees. Putnam

DURANT, JOHN. The Story of Baseball in Words and Pictures. Hastings House

LOUIS, JOE. How to Box. McKay

BUCHANAN, LAMONT. The Story of Basketball. Greenberg

JOHNSON, OWEN. The Prodigious Hickey. Little, Brown

THAYER, ERNEST L. Casey at the Bat (poem)

BROWNING, ROBERT. Pheidippides (poem)

BOND, NELSON. Mr. Mergenthwirker's Lobblies. Coward-McCann

SHEPARD, ESTHER. Paul Bunyan. Harcourt, Brace

SHAPIRO, IRWIN. John Henry and the Double-Jointed Steam-Drill. Messner

BOWMAN, JAMES C. Pecos Bill. Whitman
MONTAGUE, MARGARET. Up Eel River. Macmillan
SHAPIRO, IRWIN. Joe Magarac and his U.S.A. Citizen Papers. Messner

VERNE, JULES. Twenty Thousand Leagues Under the Sea. Scribner
WELLS, H. G. Seven Famous Novels. Knopf

SAINT-EXUPÉRY, ANTOINE DE. Night Flight. Appleton-Century
LINDBERGH, ANNE. North to the Orient. Harcourt, Brace
SHUTE, NEVIL. No Highway. Morrow
MAGEE, JOHN G., JR. High Flight (poem)

DOYLE, A. CONAN. Adventures of Sherlock Holmes. Grosset
CHESTERTON, G. K. Father Brown Omnibus. Dodd, Mead
BIGGERS, EARL. The Chinese Parrot. Grosset
CHRISTIE, AGATHA. The Murder of Roger Ackroyd. Pocket Books
BAILEY, H. C. Mr. Fortune Speaking. Dutton
STOUT, REX. And Be a Villain. Viking
FREEMAN, R. AUSTIN. Mr. Pottermack's Oversight. Dodd, Mead
SAYERS, DOROTHY. Strong Poison. Harcourt, Brace
FROME, DAVID. Mr. Pinkerton Goes to Scotland Yard. Pocket Books
WENTWORTH, PATRICIA. Eternity Ring. Lippincott
PALMER, STUART. Four Lost Ladies. Mill
COLLINS, WILKIE. The Moonstone. Dodd, Mead
POE, EDGAR ALLAN. The Murders in the Rue Morgue (in *Best Tales of Edgar Allan Poe*). Modern Library
MASON, A. E. W. At the Villa Rose. Hodder
RINEHART, MARY ROBERTS. The Circular Staircase. Rinehart
GREEN, ANNA KATHARINE. The Leavenworth Case. Putnam

FLOHERTY, JOHN J. Inside the F.B.I. Lippincott
———— Behind the Silver Shield. Lippincott
FORD, COREY. Cloak and Dagger. Grosset
GARDNER, ERLE STANLEY. The Cautious Coquette. Morrow
TRAIN, ARTHUR. Mr. Tutt Finds a Way. Scribner

WISTER, OWEN. The Virginian. Grosset

RHODES, EUGENE. The Proud Sheriff. Houghton, Mifflin
JAMES, WILL. Lone Cowboy. Scribner
——— Smoky. Scribner
FIELD, PETER. Powder Valley Showdown. Morrow
EVANS, EVAN. Montana Rides Again. Harper
COOLIDGE, DANE. Texas Cowboys. Dutton
RAINE, WILLIAM M. The Sheriff's Son. Houghton, Mifflin
LARKIN, MARGARET. Singing Cowboy. Knopf
BARNES, RUTH. I Hear America Singing. Winston
BENÉT, WILLIAM ROSE. The Horse Thief (poem)
AIKEN, CONRAD. The Kid (poem)
CODY, WILLIAM. Buffalo Bill's Life Story. Farrar
VESTAL, STANLEY. Kit Carson. Houghton, Mifflin
ROURKE, CONSTANCE. Davy Crockett. Harcourt, Brace
BUFFALO CHILD LONG LANCE. Long Lance. Rinehart
VESTAL, STANLEY. Sitting Bull. Houghton, Mifflin
BAKELESS, JOHN. Fighting Frontiersman: The Life of Daniel
    Boone. Morrow
PARKMAN, FRANCIS. The Oregon Trail. Rinehart

STEVENSON, R. L. Treasure Island. Scribner
——— Kidnapped. Scribner
ORCZY, EMMUSKA. The Scarlet Pimpernel. Putnam
DICKENS, CHARLES. Pickwick Papers. Macrae Smith
HERSEY, JOHN. A Bell for Adano. Knopf

PEASE, HOWARD. The Tattooed Man. Doubleday
CONRAD, JOSEPH. Typhoon. Doubleday
SABATINI, RAFAEL. Captain Blood. Houghton, Mifflin
VILLIERS, ALAN. The Set of the Sails. Scribner
MASEFIELD, JOHN. Dauber (poem)
HOMER. Odyssey (trans. by T. E. Shaw). Oxford

TURLEY, CHARLES. Voyages of Captain Scott. Dodd, Mead
ROOS, ANN. Man of Molokai. Lippincott
BOAS, LOUISE. A Great Rich Man. Longmans
EADIE, THOMAS. I Like Diving. Houghton, Mifflin
HOWARD, SIDNEY, Yellow Jack. Harcourt, Brace
SCOGGIN, MARGARET. The Lure of Danger. Knopf

And all my days are trances,
   And all my nightly dreams
Are where thy grey eye glances,
   And where thy footstep gleams—
In what ethereal dances,
   By what eternal streams.
          —POE, *To One in Paradise*

CHAPTER 5

Books
of Romance

ADVENTURE is not a masculine monopoly in books any more
than in life, but the preceding chapter may have left you with
the feeling that the boys in your library are being very well
looked after and the girls neglected. A great many of the books
and subjects mentioned, however, are as popular with girls as
with boys. If one were to generalize about their reading—
generalizations are never safe, however, and you'd better keep
an eye on your young people and see if there is any truth in
this—one would say that boys range more widely in their reading than girls, their interests seem broader.

Oliver Wendell Holmes had this to say about it:

*Forget
the girls?
No indeed*

I found that the difference between her reading and mine was
like that of a man's and a woman's dusting a library. The man flaps
about with a bunch of feathers; the woman goes to work softly with
a cloth. She does not raise half the dust, nor fill her eyes and mouth
with it,—but she goes into all the corners and attends to the leaves
as much as to the covers.—Books are the *negative* pictures of
thought, and the more sensitive the mind that receives their images,
the more nicely the finest lines are reproduced. A woman (of the
right kind), reading after a man, follows him as Ruth followed the
reapers of Boaz, and her gleanings are often the finest of the wheat.[1]

[1] O. W. Holmes, *Autocrat of the Breakfast Table* (Houghton, 1891),
p. 275.

That is rather flattering to the "weaker sex" than otherwise. Certainly girls are more voracious readers of fiction and imaginative works in general than boys, and as boys demand Adventure, so girls require Romance.

Love stories   The request will probably come to you simply worded: "Can you recommend a good love story?" *Can* you? Literature is full of them. But before you reach for *Romeo and Juliet*, take a good look at the girl before you. It may be that what she really wants to start with is *Big Doc's Girl* or *Date for Diane* or *Green Grass of Wyoming*. She may not even be ready for the introspection of *Seventeenth Summer* or the harrowing experiences of *Mrs. Mike*. But see to it that she sometime has the great love stories, not forgetting *Cyrano* or the endlessly beautiful poetry from "How do I love thee?" to Robinson's *Tristram*.

Romance   The novels of the Brontës with their stormy passions, the medieval richness of Sigrid Undset's *Kristin Lavransdatter*, the delicacy of Elinor Wylie's *Venetian Glass Nephew* and the strength of Willa Cather's *My Ántonia*, the haunting prose of W. H. Hudson's *Green Mansions* and the gleam of James Stephens' *Crock of Gold*—all these and more give evidence of that elusive quality called romance.

It may be historical with great exemplars from Scott to Kenneth Roberts—and since there are great ones, why should anyone bother with the lesser breed?—or it may be as contemporary as Maureen Daly's *Seventeenth Summer*; it may be as tapestried as Charles Reade's *Cloister and the Hearth* or as bare of ornament as Caroline's own little house in Rose Wilder Lane's *Let the Hurricane Roar*; it may be as foreign as *Anna Karenina* or as familiar as *Winter Wheat*; sad or joyous or serene; but always there is a quickening of the pulse as one reads and a glimpse of life heightened by emotion.

Isn't this guidance, too?   And since emotion is a prime factor here, it is important that the books selected shall portray emotion faithfully, shall not be spurious or artificial, and that the characters have life and respond truly to life situations. As with all books for young people, no reader should be left with a sense of the futility of existence. If the book is an historical novel, it must show respect for the facts of history and portray both the characters and the period with fidelity, though the scholarship that validates it must keep its place in the background. If it is contemporary life that is being depicted, it should have recognizable reality and more than surface reflections.

Through these books, written with the insight and the impact that the imaginative writer can give, characters become "larger than human," and life itself seems luminous. One often learns more about oneself and one's fellows, about the potentialities and the inequities of human society through reading fiction than through factual books or even through everyday living. Such novels need not be primarily psychological or sociological; often they are not, but if they are novels of any depth, they are bound to deal with these matters. It is imperative, therefore, that they do not emphasize false values. This does not mean that every character must be saintly or that life's rawness must be kept hidden, but only that the legitimate hopes and expectancies of youth should not be betrayed.

Pleaders for naturalism in literature may try to persuade you, "But they are not seeing Life; *this* is Life!" Is it? Is it all of life? Or is it, as the satirist would say, "life as it is but as it should not be"?

This is not to say that youth must keep its illusions, though every confirmed lover of life must at times feel that even the extravagancies of youth are nearer to the heart of the matter than the bitterness of the cynic. "It takes life to love Life." Some of us oldsters are wise enough to realize what benefits accrue to us from consorting with the young and seeing life through their eyes. Others try to disguise the fact by an attempt at objectivity and talk about the necessity for working with young people in the community "because they will be the citizens of tomorrow." That is a puny argument, looking hopefully to the retention of our own political, social, and economic ideas, an attempt to abdicate our own responsibilities and postpone decisive action for a generation. We should stay on the job but call on youth as an added inspiration and resource, make use of its eagerness, its alertness, its undauntedness, its tirelessness to instill fresh hope into our own "practicality" and jaded thinking—a powerful pressure group against our own inertia. Youth has much to contribute, not by being tomorrow's voters but by being young today. We need their "audacity of belief."

Don't worry too much   They look at the world with clear and steady and rather sharp eyes, the young people of this generation. They do not shy away from controversial issues in life or in their reading or ask to have the facts disguised. So don't you. And don't worry too much. There are a good many books in your library that you'd probably prefer them not to read. You think young people haven't the requisite maturity to cope with them, and perhaps they haven't. But how does maturity come? Through years only? Or through experience? And aren't we counting on books to give certain experiences we ourselves don't undergo? These young people can stand shocks. Every step in the process of growing up is a shock. Still they want to grow up, *and we want them to grow up*. As for books that go into too lavish or clinical details or are marked by profanity or lewd language, if they are in your library, you cannot keep them from young people without making them seem additionally alluring. But if they are in your library, presumably they have something to commend them, and even youthful readers may be able to discover what that something is.

They sometimes react violently to such reading, these young people, closing a book after a chapter or two with disgust and a dark disapproval of their elders, for youth can be priggish. Sometimes they accept it resignedly as the mood of today. Sometimes they shrug it off, as if wondering why any human being should be so lacking in intelligence or force. Their reaction never seems to be, "This might happen to me," but rather, "*I'd* never be like that!" As for a world in which the cards seem to be stacked, that's one of the things they expect to change.

A steady diet of this reading, unrelieved by any books that testify to the joy and beauty and wonder of life, would be frightful for any of us to contemplate. That is where *you* come in with your ready understanding of anyone who wants to know what life is really like and your ability to suggest books that should justly be read along with the others.

All this was said with such sagacity some years ago that it would be a pity not to repeat it here:

Nearly everything that happens in novels had happened in the village where I grew up. Here were romance and mystery, beauty and terror, here lived cowards, liars, thieves, and adulterers, as well as men and women of character and definite achievement. I had seen with my own eyes, heard with my own ears and felt with strong feelings of my own the human drama in which I was playing a part long before I was fifteen.

A frank determination to know all that can happen to human beings in books or in life is quite different from a prurient curiosity. Feeling under the obligation myself, I have never been shocked to find other boys and girls similarly impelled to find out all that they can. Tragedy lies, I think, not in knowing too much but rather in not knowing enough to think things through.[2]

There are bound to be some girls and boys, as there are some adults, who read for greedy relish of sordid details. Do not let them set the pace for the rest but try to straighten out that perversity by frank discussion. Sometimes books on psychology, written for youthful consumption, will help.

Most vital, in this connection, is it that your own thinking be mature and liberal and unprejudiced, your own reading, wide, and your own personality, one that is acceptable to young people.

[2] From *My Roads to Childhood* by Anne Carroll Moore, copyright 1939. Used by permission of Doubleday & Company, Inc.

You know the one thing that would probably help more than anything else? A sense of humor. It keeps one in balance.

And now to return to some of youth's reading enjoyments.

Fantasy   There is a sort of secret joy to be found in the reading of phantasmagoria—those tales that are not quite of this earth and air, that transcend the limitations of time and space. Books like Robert Nathan's *Portrait of Jennie* or Elswyth Thane's *Tryst* or James Hilton's *Lost Horizon* have that linking of the real with what must be unreal and yet seems just around the corner in discovery and comprehension. There is fun in letting the centuries merge, as they do in Mark Twain's *Connecticut Yankee in King Arthur's Court* or in Balderston's fine play, *Plays*   *Berkeley Square*. Several plays hold a gleam of this fantastic light: Barrie's *Dear Brutus*, Maxwell Anderson's *High Tor*, Thornton Wilder's *Our Town*, George S. Kaufman's *Beggar on Horseback*, to name only a few. You must certainly have plays in your collection for both reading and production, and, if you are lucky enough to have a clubroom at the disposal of your young people, I hope you can collect duplicates of some of the most enjoyable plays so that there can be evenings spent in reading plays aloud together. Don't try to find star performers, don't rehearse, don't even suggest anyone's reading in advance; just let the crowd sit around in a circle, start anywhere with the first character to appear, and let the next person in the circle assume the next role. Be ready, yourself, to fill in with stage directions or explanations if and when needed. Barrie's play, *Shall We Join the Ladies?*, would be a beguiling one to begin with. If some of your young people are having difficulty getting started in reading plays, this business of reading parts together, reading aloud, will be sure to help.

Although drama is a distinct form of writing and will probably be shelved by itself, it is a mistake to exclude it in your thinking from the subject matter with which it naturally allies itself. Characters and incidents from plays should inject themselves into discussions as naturally as fictional or historical personages. When life itself is being explored, what matters the form in which the answers come?

The fun of discovering one's self—and a helpful form of reading for you as a young people's librarian, by the way—may come from reading about another person of similar age and problems: *Alice Adams*, Peter in *Fortitude*, Minoche in *The Broken Arc*, Arthur in *Ah, Wilderness*, the young people in Rumer Godden's books, *The River* and *A Candle for St. Jude*, Page in *The Fair Adventure*, or Jody in *The Yearling*. It may come from glimpses of remembered youth in autobiographical writing or fiction based on family recollections: *Out on a Limb, We Shook the Family Tree, One Foot in Heaven, Dune Boy, Midway in My Song, West with the Night, Syrian Yankee*. It may suddenly flash upon one in a reading of "Renascence" or "Reluctance" or "The Ballad of East and West" or "The Last Ride Together" or *The People, Yes*. Sandburg has said, "The test of a poem is never 'Do I understand it?' but 'What has it done to me?' "; and poetry can open many doors for young people that we may never know about. *Mirror for adolescents*

The same is true for the essay, which is very close to poetry in its power of reflection and revelation: *Life's Minor Collisions, In Our Convent Days, Mince Pie, The River Pasture, The Private Papers of Henry Ryecroft*—these not only uncover queer quirks in ourselves but establish a contemplative mood in which we often find ourselves formulating essays of our own in our minds. Encourage your young people in their natural tendencies toward the keeping of diaries or journals and of jotting down thoughts as they occur to them without waiting for stipulated times. *Essays*

Not only knowledge of self comes through these channels, a dawning recognition of what makes us individual ("I am a part of all that I have met"), but knowledge of others, some indication of how humans manage to get along together, of what basic similarities bring us together in spite of our surface differences;

The brotherhood is not by the blood certainly.
But neither are men brothers by speech—by saying so;
Men are brothers by life lived and are hurt for it.[3]

Books of foreign countries, fiction and nonfiction alike, testify to the truth of MacLeish's verse: *Unveiled; The Family; East Wind, West Wind; A World Can End; Cry, the Beloved Country; Home to India; Days of Ofelia.* These are books that may need introducing to your young people, for the first inclination is toward the near at hand and the familiar rather than the cosmopolitan; but once introduced, books like these become accepted companions. And if no books needed introducing, where in the world would your job be?

The important—and difficult—thing is to know by intuition or to learn through trial and error how to introduce what to whom—and when.

Of this, more later.

Books mentioned in this chapter

SHAKESPEARE, WILLIAM. Romeo and Juliet
MEDEARIS, MARY. Big Doc's Girl. Lippincott
HEADLEY, ELIZABETH. Date for Diane. Macrae Smith
O'HARA, MARY. Green Grass of Wyoming. Lippincott
FREEDMAN, BENEDICT. Mrs. Mike. Coward-McCann
ROSTAND, EDMOND. Cyrano de Bergerac (trans. by Brian Hooker). Holt
BROWNING, ELIZABETH. Sonnets from the Portuguese. Harper
ROBINSON, E. A. Tristram. Macmillan

BRONTË, CHARLOTTE. Jane Eyre. Oxford
BRONTË, EMILY. Wuthering Heights. Random House
UNDSET, SIGRID. Kristin Lavransdatter. Knopf
WYLIE, ELINOR. The Venetian Glass Nephew. Knopf
CATHER, WILLA. My Ántonia. Houghton, Mifflin
HUDSON, W. H. Green Mansions. Grosset
STEPHENS, JAMES. Crock of Gold. Macmillan

[3] From "Speech to Those Who Say Comrade" in *Public Speech,* copyright 1936 by Archibald MacLeish. Reprinted by permission of Rinehart & Company, Inc., publishers.

SCOTT, WALTER. The Talisman. McKay
ROBERTS, KENNETH. Rabble in Arms. Doubleday
DALY, MAUREEN. Seventeenth Summer. Dodd, Mead
READE, CHARLES. The Cloister and the Hearth. Dodd, Mead
LANE, ROSE WILDER. Let the Hurricane Roar. Longmans
TOLSTOI, LEO. Anna Karenina. Macrae Smith
WALKER, MILDRED. Winter Wheat. Harcourt, Brace

NATHAN, ROBERT. Portrait of Jennie. Knopf
THANE, ELSWYTH. Tryst. Harcourt, Brace
HILTON, JAMES. Lost Horizon. Morrow
CLEMENS, SAMUEL L. A Connecticut Yankee in King Arthur's
    Court. Harper
BALDERSTON, J. L. Berkeley Square. Macmillan
BARRIE, JAMES M. Dear Brutus. Scribner
ANDERSON, MAXWELL. High Tor. Dodd, Mead
WILDER, THORNTON. Our Town. Coward-McCann
KAUFMAN, GEORGE S. Beggar on Horseback. Liveright
BARRIE, JAMES M. Shall We Join the Ladies? (in his *Plays*).
    Scribner

TARKINGTON, BOOTH. Alice Adams. Grosset
WALPOLE, HUGH. Fortitude. Modern Library
MEYNENG, MAYETTE. The Broken Arc. Harper
O'NEILL, EUGENE. Ah, Wilderness. Random House
GODDEN, RUMER. The River. Little, Brown
——— A Candle for St. Jude. Viking
GRAY, ELIZABETH J. The Fair Adventure. Viking
RAWLINGS, MARJORIE. The Yearling. Scribner
BAKER, LOUISE. Out on a Limb. McGraw-Hill
DOLSON, HILDEGARDE. We Shook the Family Tree. Random House
SPENCE, HARTZELL. One Foot in Heaven. McGraw-Hill
TEALE, EDWIN WAY. Dune Boy. Dodd, Mead

LEHMANN, LOTTE. Midway in My Song. Bobbs-Merrill
MARKHAM, BERYL. West with the Night. Houghton, Mifflin
RIZK, SALOM. Syrian Yankee. Doubleday
MILLAY, EDNA ST. VINCENT. Renascence (poem)
FROST, ROBERT. Reluctance (poem)
KIPLING, RUDYARD. The Ballad of East and West (poem)

BROWNING, ROBERT. The Last Ride Together (poem)
SANDBURG, CARL. The People, Yes (poem). Harcourt, Brace

WARNER, FRANCES LESTER. Life's Minor Collisions. Houghton, Mifflin
REPPLIER, AGNES. In Our Convent Days. Houghton, Mifflin
MORLEY, CHRISTOPHER. Mince Pie. Lippincott
VAN DER VEER, JUDY. The River Pasture. Longmans
GISSING, GEORGE. The Private Papers of Henry Ryecroft. Dutton

EKREM, SELMA. Unveiled. Ives Washburn
FEDEROVA, NINA. The Family. Little, Brown
BUCK, PEARL. East Wind, West Wind. John Day
SKARIATINA, IRINA. A World Can End. Random House
PATON, ALAN. Cry, the Beloved Country. Scribner
RAMA RAU, SANTHA. Home to India. Harper
DIAMANT, GERTRUDE. Days of Ofelia. Houghton, Mifflin

And who made 'em? Who made the skyscrapers?
Man made 'em, the little two-legged joker, Man.
Out of his head, out of his dreaming, scheming skypiece,
Out of proud little diagrams that danced softly in his head—
Man made the skyscrapers.

—SANDBURG, *Good Morning, America*

CHAPTER 6

Books
on How-to-do-it

IT WOULD BE surprising if young people growing up in a country that prides itself on its "know-how" should not take an interest in the how-to-do-it books, and if the boys and girls in your library are not looking for books on the technique of everything from electronics to dancing, they must be in a class by themselves. These are the books that must be kept up to the minute, discarded and replaced as fashions change and technology advances. The boy who wants to build his own radio set or model airplane will want to incorporate the most recent findings; your copies of official rules for all sports must be replaced whenever new ones appear; vocational material may well be sought in pamphlets as well as books; and, as a matter of fact, pamphlet material and magazines will be an important part of your young people's collection. There are reputable houses dealing with vocational pamphlets[1] and with current events (Headline Series, for instance), not to mention the scores of government bulletins that will be useful—those on the national parks, on agriculture, and on home economics and decoration, for example.

"Know-how"

[1] Listed in *Subscription Books Bulletin* (January 1944 and January 1945), and in Gertrude Forrester, *Occupational Pamphlets* (H. W. Wilson Co., 1948).

Hobbies   The "hobby" shelf should reflect every interest of your young people, and attractive, frequently changed exhibits which include examples of their work will enliven and advertise it. True, a great many people work at crafts with no thought of books, no feeling of need for their assistance. It is for you to uncover to them the wealth of information books hold or the amusing and helpful accounts people like themselves have written on how their own hobbies have possessed them.

Young people somehow never think of adults at play, especially adults whose minds are occupied with weighty matters, and for them to hear of all the gadgets Thomas Jefferson was everlastingly strewing about his house or of John Muir inventing a bed that would get him up in the mornings and a desk that would apportion his time among various studies is often to get an entirely new view of people and a new approach to books. So watch out for these instances as they appear while you read and pigeonhole them for future reference.

Books on magic never stay very long on the shelves; neither do books on scientific experiments. You will probably have, somewhere in your library, reference copies of books for the collectors: stamps, coins, etc. They should be available for young people as well as for adults. The Leeming *Fun with . . .* books may look too young for your purpose, but they are not. It is wise to have some of the simpler and clearly illustrated books. Look for those that deal with inexpensive or easily obtained materials, for those that contain challenging ideas and send the reader off on his own, for those that can be immediately put to work—room decoration, gift making, etc. Boys and girls who still have difficulty with the printed page may find such books an opening wedge to reading, and, as they learn to turn the pages easily in their search for directions and illustrations, they will be overcoming some of their fear and hostility toward books.

How to be   Books on etiquette and on the whole matter of growing up
an adult   are among the most desired items, but they are seldom asked

for. Don't let the apparent lack of demand mislead you. Acquire a few of the best written, most practical, and most wholesome books and leave them around in plain view. Books in this category should deal with the kind of living represented in your community; as a rule, young people are not interested in the layout of silver and glass for millionaires' banquets. The writing in these books should be neither flippant nor stodgy; line drawings and cartoons are excellent additions to the text and conveyors of ideas on their own.

The bothersome question will arise: what to do about books on sex education? There is no doubt that young people want them, and since there are such excellent books available as Strain's *Teen Days* and Keliher's *Life and Growth* it is too bad there should be even a question about providing them. One is usually governed somewhat in the matter by the attitude of the community. Some libraries keep such books on open shelves; many others keep them on closed shelves but give them out to young people without question when requests are made.

Some "how-to-do-it" books have already been suggested in the chapter dealing with books of adventure—technical accounts of sports, aviation, etc. Reference should be made to them again so that they will not be forgotten. When it comes to science, *Science* the list takes on sizable proportions. Not only is there interest in scientific experiments but in such explanatory writing as *Physics Tells Why* and *Understanding Science*. (It is dangerous to give titles; they date so quickly.) Through the alphabet, from agronomy, anatomy, anthropology, archeology, astronomy, geology, meteorology, and paleontology to zoology, you will find fascinating subjects for young people to explore, if only you can supply them with readable books, and in many of these fields there are readable books to be had. The average librarian, it must be confessed, is not particularly well grounded in science, and it is entirely possible that books we consider too technical and difficult and advanced would seem eminently "readable" to the young. Tribute to young people's familiarity with scientific data comes from a source that will be particularly welcome to them:

On the night of August 6th [this was in 1945] before the atom bomb took complete charge, there was a brief suspended moment whose unfamiliar sweetness we savored with a satisfaction untroubled by the foreknowledge of doom. For a few hours that summer night, several million American boys and girls of around sixteen suddenly rose to undreamed of heights in their own households, as they deftly took the conversation away from their fumbling parents and from the radio and, in lucid, painstaking, and charitably simple language, interpreted the atom to their elders. The necessary introductions which were performed courteously and with hardly any patronizing, could have been made by no more competent authorities. Although it seemed as if it would shortly be followed by the end of the world, the evening was indisputably a triumph.[2]

The excellent writing in recent years on the subject of medicine—biographical and fictional as well as descriptive and explanatory—has led to an increased interest in and demand for such material. And fortunately you can always count upon a steady request from girls for information about nursing, both vocational and fictional. In these fields, also, it is most important that your collection be kept up to date in recording discoveries.

Vocations   Perhaps a word should be said in favor of vocational books in general lest earlier mention of the use of pamphlet material lead you to consider books unnecessary. Several good surveys of occupational fields should be at hand, showing the scope of work and the general qualifications for it, even if such matters as opportunities and remuneration have to be omitted—books like Davey's *Everyday Occupations* and Huff's *Twenty Careers of Tomorrow*. A great many young people have no more leaning toward one vocation than another. They need exploratory books, straightforward, factual information, gathered by repre-

[2] By permission. Copyright 1945, The New Yorker Magazine, Inc.

sentative workers or by experts in the field of vocational guidance. They need biographical and fictional material sometimes
to rouse dormant or unsuspected interests, but you should be
sure that the career stories you select are not the poor-boy-to-
riches type.

"Career"
stories

You may be impressed by the popularity of "career" stories
with young people, but do not attribute all of it to their concern
with occupations. These books present contemporary life and
are written in easy narrative style with an occasional touch
of romance. The "career" becomes at times of less importance.
If these stories do not hold up as stories, do not meet the
standards you set for other books of fiction, don't bother with
them because of their vocational content.

Vocational guidance is too specialized a field for a librarian to
blunder into nor should she consider it as part of her work
unless she has had professional training for it. But at least she
can provide accurate and stimulating printed information as
it is needed.

The how-to-do-it books extend even into the territory of the
fine arts—how to make musical instruments, how to whittle
and carve and draw and paint and write. Books on cartooning
and caricature are popular and they are helpful if you wish to
discuss the background, possibilities and limitations of so-called
"comics." Books on puppetry and model-theater craft may
develop an interest in drama, or a demand for them may pro-
ceed from such an interest. Journalism is another subject
popular with young people. And what shall be said of photography, of radio and television? Not only is there interest in
the making and repair of sets, but in the scientific principles
underlying wireless and in the possibilities of the profession
from engineer to script writer and performer.

Back
to guidance

All of these interests provide you with occasion for introducing
books in the subject areas: biographies of musicians, artists,
writers, and so on. Learn to enliven every subject as it comes
along with books drawn from various sections of your shelves.

I should never let any musically interested person, for instance, fail to see *People of Note*, hilarious verses and drawings about the members of the symphony orchestra.

There's more to be said on this matter of associating books, and we should get around to it in another chapter or two.

Books mentioned in this chapter

LISITZKY, GENE. Thomas Jefferson. Viking

MUIR, JOHN. Story of My Boyhood and Youth. Houghton, Mifflin

LEEMING, JOSEPH. Fun with . . . . Lippincott

STRAIN, FRANCES. Teen Days. Appleton-Century
KELIHER, ALICE. Life and Growth. Appleton-Century

LUHR, OVERTON. Physics Tells Why. Cattell
CROUSE, WILLIAM. Understanding Science. Whittlesey House

DAVEY, MILDRED. Everyday Occupations. Heath
HUFF, DARRELL. Twenty Careers of Tomorrow. Whittlesey House

McKINNEY, LAURENCE. People of Note. Dutton

My long two-pointed ladder's sticking through a tree
Toward heaven still,
And there's a barrel that I didn't fill
Beside it, and there may be two or three
Apples I didn't pick upon some bough.
But I am done with apple-picking now.

—FROST, *After Apple-picking*

CHAPTER 7

And Others

BOOKS OF adventure and of romance do more than reflect life; they illumine it. Along with the quasi-technical books discussed in the preceding chapter, they can give young people a pretty good idea of where they are going and what they are doing. They do not complete the picture of young people's reading, however, and in order to do that, it may be well to revert to the four main reasons for reading (Chapter 2) and note what further interests are evoked. And so let us go back, first, to curiosity.

The curiosity of a child is all-embracing and omnipresent. *Curiosity* Adults worry if it is not, despite the fact that respites from a constant bombardment of searching questions are greeted with enormous sighs of relief. By the time one reaches the teens, however, he is more guarded in his inquiries and more specialized in his interests. He has begun to adopt the pattern of his group and to shrink within its circumference. Pressures of everyday living—the well-known "shades of the prison-house"—tend to confine rather than to broaden his outlook. And yet he looks out upon the world with eagerness and a wide ranging mind. The explorer has not yet disappeared from his make-up.

He hears all about best sellers and expects them not only to *The* keep him in touch with all other followers of the latest fancy, *contemporary* but to spread before him the contemporary scene with some insight into its workings. He reads the journalists and foreign correspondents with the same expectation, listens to news commentators on the radio, watches the "March of Time" and similar programs in the movies. His favorite magazines, according to surveys of young people's reading,[1] are *Life* and the *Reader's Digest*, both of which specialize in mirroring the contemporary. Because he is exposed to all the mass media of communication, he is aware of such diverse domestic issues as housing, civil rights, soil erosion, unions, public utilities, etc., and cognizant of problems facing the rest of the world. No country seems far away, now that its troubles impinge directly upon our own, its representatives (in the United Nations) are in our midst, and every community boasts its share of men who have served their country in every theater of war and returned to tie more tightly the cords that bind us all together. The menace of atomic energy is not forgotten by young people, nor the urgency of finding solutions that will permit its development for purposes other than war.

Books on all of these subjects, not "written down" for the teen ager but couched in the everyday accents he readily understands, are as essential to your collection as they are to his mental growth. And he reads them, not as a conscious form of education, but to satisfy the curiosity and desire for information which accompany his development. Since personal interests usually come first, however, in adolescence—absorption in the self and its immediate concerns—it may be well for us to see to it that the larger scene is not forgotten and to revive or stimulate in every way and by every means possible the curiosity that will lead to such reading.

Pictorial books like *The River, American Counterpoint*, and the *American Annual of Photography* are eye-catchers and seemingly made for our purpose. So also are books that combine

---

[1] Marion Larbey, "Study of Recreational Magazine Reading of Young People," unpublished thesis (The New York Public Library, 1945).

excellent reporting with attractive format: *No Place to Hide*, and *Early Tales of the Atomic Age*, for example. The Gunther books, though long, do not seem formidable to young people and may usually be counted upon to touch off discussion or debate. And peculiarly appealing are books like Delia Goetz's *Other Young Americans* that show what part youth can play in his own community and in the world.

Not all of these books will be popular. Perhaps none of them will be. But they will be looked into, read piecemeal, referred to by a great many young people and devoured by others. As for best sellers and controversial books in the idiom of today, some of them should be on hand. But be selective. Neither include all nor exclude all. And buttress today's books with others that will give background and offer measuring rods.

Travel books and all writing that opens up other lands, *Travel books* whether it be history, biography, fiction, folklore, or "picture books," should be given encouragement by display and casual discussion. You must know from your own experience that such books are relished more when read *after* one has visited a place than before. With many young people, these books will have to provide a substitute for actual journeying, but I should never suggest that idea to them. They would scorn the very notion. They have their whole lives ahead of them, haven't they? Who knows *where* they'll go? (Who, indeed?) And so I should agree with them—"You'll probably be going to ———— someday. Want to see what it's like?"

If curiosity is the reason for most of the reading done by young people, as well as ourselves, it is also the factor we play upon in stimulating wide reading. We make use of it in book talks or in floor work, not by saying archly "If you want to know what happened next, read the book!" but certainly by implying it. That technique works well with readers of normal attainment. For the one with reading difficulty, it is not so successful. He will read with much more zest and interest if he is told even more about the story. A touch of sureness is added to his approach and confidence in the book given him. But the fact that suspense is not an important element in his reading does not mean that curiosity is lacking in his make-up. He is curious about many things, and if you can convince him that books hold the answers to many of the questions that torment him, he may learn to use books as tools long before he feels any pleasure in reading as such. Perhaps the only thing he wants to know about at the moment is how to raise rabbits, and it would never occur to him to go to a *library* to find out. We must constantly remind ourselves that to many people the library is still an institution devoted solely to scholarly research. Teen agers who have never had the experience of "belonging" to a children's room seldom have any idea of the interest the public library takes in their welfare and the resources it is ready to put at their disposal. Once they realize that the facilities of public institutions develop in answer to expressed and evident public needs, that they themselves are part of that public, and that librarians welcome their opinions, they are more than ready to state them.

Magazines   Young people throughout the country, for instance, in answer to a library survey made in 1945, listed the following magazines as most popular with them, in the following order:

Life	*Calling All Girls*
Reader's Digest	*Woman's Home Companion*
Seventeen	*National Geographic*
Saturday Evening Post	*Time*
Ladies' Home Journal	*Popular Mechanics*
Popular Science	*Coronet*
Good Housekeeping	*Look*
tied { *Colliers*	*New Yorker*
Vogue	*Newsweek*
Mademoiselle	*Cosmopolitan*

But when one young people's library, in considering its annual order for periodicals, asked what other magazines would be useful, excellent suggestions poured in: *Band Leaders, Baseball,*

Air Force, Modern Screen, Metronome, among others.

Magazines seem to be pretty popular with all young people. For the most part, they are lively in appearance with short articles that do not exhaust a normal span of attention and sprinkled with advertising that has an undeniable appeal. The stories they contain are read also, although the same young people who read them will tell you they don't like short stories. The fact that they read short stories avidly in magazines and object to them in books is just one of their minor inconsistencies that never seem to bother them.

A glance through the names of the magazines listed will remind us that young people read for relaxation as well as to satisfy curiosity. They pick up books too that require no special mental effort, that are, in fact, not far removed from the stories they enjoyed at 10 or 12 years of age. The so-called "girl's stories" enter here, and, although some of them seem too juvenile to be admitted to collections that are predominantly adult, still they have their uses there. They ease the path to the adult novel. They reassure the immature and the retarded readers who feel that they have gone beyond their depth. There are good wholesome stories in this field, some of them extremely well written and pleasant to look back upon even when one has outgrown them, Elizabeth Janet Gray's *The Fair Adventure,* for example. The same is true of boys' books, the Pease and Meader type, or even some as young as Armstrong Sperry's books.

Another class of books thoroughly enjoyed by both boys and girls is the one dealing with animals—fact and fiction, wild and domesticated. Sometimes the appealing factor is the flattering devotion of one's four-legged companion, as in the Terhune books; sometimes the thrill of savage kinship, as in *Call of the Wild*; or the sense of actual danger in *Man-Eaters of Kumaon* and Buck's *Bring 'Em Back Alive.* Lumped together as "animal stories," such books strike an offensively juvenile note and may be considered beneath the dignity of a teen ager. But if you speak of books about horses or dogs or tigers, the reaction is

Relaxation

Girls' stories

Boys' books

Animal life

quite different. One would think the librarian had been about to recommend Thornton Burgess, but if it's Jack London—that's different! Books on animal psychology and the care and training of pets will also be in demand if they are visible.

Humor   To have a thoroughly relaxed time, however, what is better than a bit of humor? Not joke books: they make deadly reading. But the humor that accompanies speech and informs character is a quality to be cherished, and young people are quick to show their appreciation of it. After all, they are at the age when humor is a wonderful emollient and also at the age when they themselves are the great producers, purveyors, and consumers of it. They love practical jokes; they enjoy 'ribbing' by whatever name it goes; they have spells of the giggles over seemingly nothing at all; they are ready to pay a quarter for a dime's worth of fun anytime; they relish jokes, even on themselves; they pay homage to the madcap who is "the life of the party." It would be strange indeed if all this gusto disappeared when they turned to books.

They love the effervescent youthful heroines of some of their stories who aren't necessarily cracking jokes all the time but seem bent on getting into situations. *My Sister Eileen* is a character who can always be counted upon to keep the company stirred up. I doubt if there are masculine counterparts. Willie Baxter may come nearest to it, but the humor of *Seventeen* is more apparent to an adult than to a teen ager, who's a bit uncomfortable about it. As for family situations, they started getting funny in *Life with Father* and continued in *You Can't Take It with You*, and now each year seems to add a few more instances. George Papishvily's hilarious experiences in *Anything Can Happen* and the confusion attendant upon *The Education of H*Y*M*A*N* *K*A*P*L*A*N* provide brilliant additions for young people's delight.

The "deadpan" form of humor is relished also: tall tales told solemnly as true, Benchley's "Treasurer's Report," Stephen Leacock's "With the Photographer," almost anything of Thurber's, and outrageous situations such as obtain in *Arsenic and Old Lace* and permeate all of P. G. Wodehouse's books. Wit is recognized and greeted with a shout, and satire, like *Of Thee I Sing,* for example, is highly respected and enjoyed.

Humor is a great weapon. William Rose Benét lauds it for defense:

> He fought for his soul, and the stubborn fighting
>   Tried hard his strength.
> "One needs seven souls for this new requiting,"
>   He said at length.
>
> "Six times have I come where my first hope jeered me
>   And laughed me to scorn;
> But now I fear as I never have feared me
>   To fall forsworn. . . ."
>
> "This is beyond all battles' soreness!"
>   Then his wonder cried;
> For Laughter, with shield and steely harness
>   Stood up at his side.[2]

But it may also be used for attacking. It lowers the defenses of the wary and puts them off their guard. One can often overcome the prejudice some young people have toward poetry by quoting several humorous poems, and then, when tensions are relaxed and the mood unsuspecting, slipping in some dangerously beautiful ones. A word of warning: don't ever try doing this unless you yourself thoroughly enjoy humorous verse. If you look down upon it and make use of it simply to further other ends, that disdain will be apparent and your complacent plans ruined. Allies such as F. P. A., Tom Daly, Arthur Guiterman, Walter Hard, A. P. Herbert, Phyllis McGinley, Ogden Nash, Dorothy Parker, *et al.* are not to be despised, nor such anthologies as McCord's *What Cheer* and Adams' *Innocent Merriment.*

Humorous poetry

---

[2] From "The Last Ally" in *Man Possessed,* copyright 1927 by William Rose Benét. Reprinted by permission of Harold Ober Associates.

"*Play in* ⠀⠀⠀⠀But it is not only humorous poetry or light verse that carries
poetry"⠀⠀⠀overtones of playfulness and badinage. In the most serious and
beautiful poetry, one is suddenly aware of a flash of light that
reveals the artist at play with his materials. Never think the
poet is not conscious of what he is doing with words:

> But word shall call to tilted word, and straighten,
> as when two spans of a bridge clap, into a line.[3]

> Indeed the whole excited town
> glowed like a shy, delicious noun,
> when some great poet lets it live
> at last beside its adjective.[4]

Words are all he has to work with—or to play with—and the
way he can make them march or dance or lag and stumble is
the measure by which he moves us.

> Lord, thy most pointed pleasure take
> And stab my spirit broad awake,[5]

cried Stevenson, and the words of poets have that piercing
quality that can penetrate directly to our emotions. As great as
their power to arouse is their magic to lull:

> You make a little foursquare block of air,
> Quiet and light and warm, in spite of all
> The illimitable dark and cold and storm.[6]

That is what the poet does. Sometimes the "little foursquare
block of air" is only four lines, sometimes a psalm or a sonnet

⠀⠀⠀[3] From "Song" in *This Blind Rose* by Humbert Wolfe, copyright 1929.
Used by permission of Doubleday & Company, Inc.
⠀⠀⠀[4] From "The Bluecoat Boy" in *Cursory Rhymes* by Humbert Wolfe,
copyright 1927. Used by permission of Doubleday & Company, Inc.
⠀⠀⠀[5] R. L. Stevenson, "The Celestial Surgeon," in his *Complete Poems*
(Scribner, 1923).
⠀⠀⠀[6] From *Complete Poems of Robert Frost*, 1949, copyright 1916, 1930,
1950 by Henry Holt and Company, Inc., copyright 1944 by Robert Frost.
Used by permission of the publishers.

or an ode, but this uncanny ability to put words in such juxta-
position as to make a phrase seem inevitable and ancient as
time itself is indeed marvelous in our eyes. We completely
forget the poet, so free is his creation from any sense of being
man-wrought. It is as if it had been put into our hands to play
with, to interpret according to the richness or the poverty of
our own experience and imagination. We carry on the play.
We carry in our memory (unconsciously, to a great extent)
verses that have struck home to us at just the right moment.
They are ours. We have earned the right to them. And once in
a while, we take them out and count them over, reveling in
our resources. We are like the boy in "The Ballad of the Harp
Weaver," who can scarcely believe his eyes:

> "She's made it for a king's son,"
> I said, "and not for me."
> But I knew it was for me.[7]

And so we take over line upon line and quote them for our
own purposes. Did Frost intend to describe the poet when he
wrote,

> You make a little foursquare block of air,
> Quiet and light and warm, in spite of all
> The illimitable dark and cold and storm.

No; he was describing the power a man and woman have to
make a home and all it connotes. But who can exhaust the
meaning a poet packs into his phrases? And so the reader has a
right to play with them and apply them in other contexts.
"The poet," said Virginia Woolf, "is always our contemporary."
That is gloriously true, for all poetry is timeless. But the poet is
more than our contemporary; he is the live coal from off the
altar that can unseal our lips. He gives us words for poetic
experiences that come upon us unawares and leave us shaken

---

[7] Edna St. Vincent Millay, title poem in her *The Harp Weaver and
Other Poems* (Harper, copyright 1922 by Edna St. Vincent Millay), p. 29.

by their beauty or their majesty. And thus he frees us to taste life to the utmost.

Young people and poetry

This alone is sufficient to commend him to young people who know all too well the feeling of paucity of language when the big moments come. Not that they consciously seek out poetry for this reason. Sometimes they are inveigled into reading it by a slim delectable volume that slips easily into the pocket, like A *Shropshire Lad* or *Second April*. Sometimes the temptation comes through a good anthology that presents subjects of their own choice, such as *Poems for a Machine Age*. Once in a while, original attempts at versifying and the desire to know how it's done lead them to Auslander and Hill's *Winged Horse* or Mearns's *Creative Youth* or Untermeyer's *Forms of Poetry*. But I think that back of these more obvious attractions, there are two forces at work impelling young people toward poetry without their knowledge or design: the necessity for breaking into brave, impossible speech drives them to seek words at their noblest and strongest; and the hunger for beauty—as fundamental as the desire for harmony in music or for a pattern in one's life—inevitably leads them where they can "hear her massive sandal set on stone." These two qualities, strength and beauty, they have a right to expect from poetry; and they do not look for them in vain, for poetry is both heroically and exquisitely fashioned.

Necessity

What can you do to help your young people enjoy poetry? Steep yourself in it, so that the anthologies and other volumes of verse on your shelves are thoroughly familiar to you. Let them be the best anthologies, too—Palgrave's *Golden Treasury*, Quiller-Couch's *Oxford Book of English Verse*, Untermeyer's *Modern American Poetry* and its companion volume *Modern British Poetry*, and Yeats's *Oxford Book of Modern Verse*. And read it aloud, to yourself alone if need be, so that you'll not be afraid of the sound of your own voice speaking it in everyday accents. The poet's eye may well be, as Shakespeare would have us believe, in a fine frenzy rolling, but anyone who speaks of poetry to young people soon learns that his own eye must be still, his voice steady. The approach should be that of everyday, no separation here, no striving to make of poetry a thing apart from life. And why, in the name of all that is sane, should we so segregate it, when it is compounded of man's experience.

> . . . woven of human joys and cares,
> Washed marvellously with sorrow, swift to mirth.[8]

This "stained-glass" attitude has done much to foster an unthinking dislike for poetry. A high school boy who had suffered from such methods retaliated with a triolet, beginning,

> Thank God I'm still plebian,
> It's easy on my mind!

One's sympathy goes out to him instinctively. As if poetry could not walk abroad in the garish light of day, as if it were in fact too bright and good for human nature's daily food! No, says your 15-year-old, it is not only ambition that should be made of sterner stuff! We break faith with the poets when we permit such misconceptions to arise. Poetry should be a joyful, natural, inevitable accompaniment of speech and of living. It should be permitted, as it alone can do, to set free the spirit, to give a lift to the day, to heighten the imagination, and to uncover the eternal verities. Those who fear for an adequate appreciation of poetry if accosted in the accents of everyday life may comfort themselves with the assurance that great art brings its own silences. It needs no artificially induced reverence on our part.

To serve the cause of poetry and youth requires, rather, a willingness to play with it[9] and to be patient, to learn to "touch and go," but never to grow discouraged and turn away.

> I sang a song to Rosamond Rose,
> Only the wind in the twilight knows;

[8] Reprinted by permission of Dodd, Mead & Company from "The Dead" in Collected Poems of Rupert Brooke, copyright 1915 by Dodd, Mead & Co., Inc.

[9] You will find help in orientation and great stimulus in Louis Untermeyer's Play in Poetry (Harcourt, Brace, 1938).

I sang a song to Jeanetta Jennie,
She flung from her window a silver penny;
I sang a song to Matilda May,
She took to her heels and ran away;
I sang a song to Susannah Sue,
She giggled the whole of the verses through:

But nevertheless, as sweet as I can,
I'll sing a song to Elizabeth Ann——[10]

And now we have considered again curiosity, relaxation, necessity. As for the fourth reason for reading, that of propinquity, you must realize that it is for you to provide it. See to it, therefore, that you are always "fustest with the mostest."

Books mentioned in this chapter

LORENTZ, PARE. The River. Stackpole
ALLAND, ALEXANDER. American Counterpoint. John Day
American Annual of Photography. American Photographic Pub.

BRADLEY, DAVID. No Place to Hide. Little, Brown
LANG, DANIEL. Early Tales of the Atomic Age. Doubleday
GOETZ, DELIA. Other Young Americans. Morrow
GUNTHER, JOHN. Inside U.S.A. Harper

GRAY, ELIZABETH JANET. The Fair Adventure. Viking
PEASE, HOWARD. The Jinx Ship. Sun Dial
MEADER, STEPHEN. Lumberjack. Harcourt, Brace
SPERRY, ARMSTRONG. Lost Lagoon. Doubleday

TERHUNE, ALBERT PAYSON. Lad: A Dog. Dutton
LONDON, JACK. The Call of the Wild. Macmillan
CORBETT, JIM. Man-Eaters of Kumaon. Oxford
BUCK, FRANK. Bring 'Em Back Alive. Garden City

McKENNEY, RUTH. My Sister Eileen. Harcourt, Brace
TARKINGTON, BOOTH. Seventeen. Grosset
DAY, CLARENCE. Life with Father. Knopf
HART, MOSS. You Can't Take It with You. Farrar
PAPASHVILY, GEORGE. Anything Can Happen. Harper

[10] From the title poem in A Child's Day by Walter de la Mare. Reproduced by permission of Henry Holt and Company, Inc.

Ross, Leonard Q. The Education of H*Y*M*A*N* K*A*P*-
  L*A*N*. Harcourt, Brace
Benchley, Robert. Benchley Beside Himself. Harper
Leacock, Stephen. Laugh Parade. Dodd, Mead
Thurber, James. The Thurber Carnival. Harper
Kesselring, Joseph. Arsenic and Old Lace. Random House
Wodehouse, P. G. Joy in the Morning. Doubleday
Kaufman, George S. and Ryskind, Morrie. Of Thee I Sing.
  Knopf

Adams, Franklin P. Nods and Becks. McGraw-Hill
Daly, T. A. Selected Poems. Harcourt, Brace
Guiterman, Arthur. Lyric Laughter. Dutton
Hard, Walter. Vermont Valley. Harcourt, Brace
Herbert, A. P. Laughing Ann and Other Poems. Benn
McGinley, Phyllis. Stones from a Glass House. Viking
Nash, Ogden. Selected Verse. Modern Library
Parker, Dorothy. Collected Poetry. Modern Library
McCord, David, ed. What Cheer. Coward-McCann
Adams, Franklin P., ed. Innocent Merriment. McGraw-Hill
Housman, A. E. A Shropshire Lad. Holt
Millay, Edna St. Vincent. Second April. Harper
McNeil, Horace and Stratton, C. Poems for a Machine Age.
  McGraw-Hill
Auslander, Joseph and Hill, F. E. The Winged Horse. Double-
  day
Mearns, Hughes. Creative Youth. Doubleday
Untermeyer, Louis. Forms of Poetry. Harcourt, Brace
Palgrave, Francis. Golden Treasury. Macmillan
Quiller-Couch, Sir Arthur, ed. Oxford Book of English Verse.
  Oxford
Untermeyer, Louis. Modern American Poetry. Harcourt, Brace
—— Modern British Poetry. Harcourt, Brace
Yeats, William Butler, ed. Oxford Book of Modern Verse.
  Oxford

PART THREE

TECHNIQUES

☞ Shut not your doors to me proud libraries,
For that which was lacking on all your well-fill'd shelves,
    yet needed most, I bring.
                    —WHITMAN, *Shut Not Your Doors*

Book Selection

Now, HAVING had a good look at your young people and their interests, all of which you expect to reflect in your book collection, do you want to draw up a set of procedures for yourself or working criteria for book selection? Let's take the latter first. What are the things to remember about your young people when it comes to selecting books?

Book selection

That there will be representatives of all reading levels, the slow, the normal (if there are any such), and the advanced; and of all interests, the prosaic and the poetic, the fanciful and the practical. There will be those concerned with school work and those concerned with making a living. There will be some who will quickly outstrip you in the breadth and the technicality of their reading, and others who will require time and patience before they even begin to experience pleasure and satisfaction from the printed page. For all of these there must be something, but the very multiplicity of books and the normal limitations of book budgets require that there be selection. And the expressed aim of the American Library Association is as valid today as when it was first proposed: "the best books for the greatest number at the least cost."

In your whole collection, try to have: Scope, coverage, variety, readability, and attractiveness.

This is the general idea

Scope. Start, of course, with the known interests of young people so as to set up the inviting element of familiarity. Add to this books that will broaden their interests. The idea back of this special collection is not so much to relieve your adult clientele from the annoying proximity of the younger set as to facilitate for these young people their transition to a large, sometimes a frighteningly large, collection of adult books. There should, therefore, be samples of practically everything; certainly every sizable division of the Dewey Decimal System will be represented. The preceding chapters have outlined the most important ones.

Coverage. Several different meanings are combined in this term. (1) The same subject may be presented in different forms. This follows from the breaking down of fiction and nonfiction barriers, as suggested in the previous chapters, and recommends your gathering material on a subject from factual, fictional, biographical, poetic, dramatic, and all other possible fields that add just the angle needed. (2) A few books should be available both for reference and for circulation. It is desirable that they be taken home for leisurely perusal but imperative that they be on hand for consultation, in case someone else has reached the circulation desk first. These are not primarily reference books; they may not even be considered informational. They may pertain to local interests or seasonal, but, as you work directly with your young people, you will discover what they are and you should act upon your discoveries promptly. (3) There is frequently a temptation to cover a subject—say, Sherlock Holmes—by the purchase of an omnibus volume. This may seem economical but it makes for poor distribution and, as a rule, is not so inviting in appearance as the separate volumes.

Variety. The same subject may appeal to a wide age range. Therefore it should be presented in books widely differing in treatment and in vocabulary; although for the latter, it is well to remember that when a person's interest in a subject is really aroused, he tends to read far beyond his native capacity. It stands to reason that, if your collection has scope and coverage, as described above, it is bound to have variety.

Readability. Sometimes this is a matter of format, sometimes of vocabulary, sometimes of construction. In general, prefer the concrete to the abstract, the simple to the involved, and the broken page to long, solid paragraphs. Again, consider your clientele. Readable for whom? If there are young people with reading difficulties, there should be simply written books with adult content, a difficult group to assemble.[1] (*Note:* This is not, by any devious twist of reasoning, to be interpreted as a recommendation of rewritten or watered-down classics.)

Attractiveness. Mostly a matter of format. See that the suspicion of juvenilia does not attach to a book, but by no means exclude all illustrated editions. Look for: clear type, not too small; wide margins; a sufficiently heavy paper to be opaque; and eye-catching but not blinding jackets.

Content

As for content, in *nonfiction* look for awareness of present-day discoveries and techniques, accuracy of research and of presentation, a style suitable to the content, and a certain persuasiveness of writing. In *fiction*, your care should be to select books that have vitality, either from character or incident or atmosphere, and that are true to the most fundamental concepts of life.

Are you up to the best books?

It will be wise, I suppose, to have mediocre books that will be read rather than superlative books that simply sit on the shelves. But you will be justified in spending the taxpayers' money on those finer books, if you will train yourself to introduce them to your would-be readers at the right time, if you will learn to know your young people so well that you can recommend when occasion arises and they will accept your recommendation even though the book seems to lack the accustomed immediate appeal, and if you yourself are so versed in good writing and so

[1] Valuable assistance may be found in *Gateways to Readable Books*, by Ruth Strang and others (H. W. Wilson, 1944), which not only lists a great many books of this kind for young people, with reading level indicated, but gives excellent advice in its introduction, "What makes a book easy to read?"

imbued with its quality that it becomes the most natural thing in the world for you to talk about it. One of the hindrances to the growth of literary appreciation in the library profession is the compulsion we are under to read the latest books, whatever they are, and to keep in touch with all contemporary expression, no matter how inept, in order to answer our inquiring readers. We need to extract time somehow for ourselves, to cultivate our own reading tastes, to follow our own special delights in reading.

It is good for us to remember, too, that much disservice has been done literature (poetry especially) by the air of sanctity with which we have invested it, so that "the classics" occupy a world apart. Sometimes it is because we ourselves have found them formidable and, although recommending them for others to read, we cannot bring ourselves to talk of them with the ease and informality that lighten our discussions of other books. We need to increase our acquaintance, to be more casual in our approach, and to be able to talk about them with the natural-ness we use toward the movies and the comic strip. We need to become so familiar with these books that we can—in the other sense of the phrase—be *familiar* with them. More people are lured into reading by someone's contagious enthusiasm for a book than by any number of remarks about the values of reading or the beauties of literature.

Wait!   We need patience, too, as we watch the sometimes tortuous unfolding of adolescence. Forced growth may exact its own penalty, and every stage of awareness can be so provocative, so challenging in itself, that we can afford to be patient in dealing with it. In guiding the reading of young people, one starts with the human being, wherever he is, and goes on as he goes on.

But watch!   The fact we must always keep in mind is that he *does go on*, that he isn't the same person day after day, that we can't even be sure his growth will be according to chart. We must rediscover him frequently and be alert to the opportunities he gives us.

There are writers who have so much of significance to say to your young people that the thought of its never reaching them should be a reproach to haunt your hours. After all, we have chosen to work with books because of our belief in their power. We must be constantly in touch with the sources of that power. The advice Maxwell Anderson gives in "Whatever Hope We Have" is applicable to us:

. . . if you practice an art, be proud of it, and make it proud of you. . . . turn to the art which has moved you most readily, take what part in it you can, as participant, spectator, secret practitioner, or hanger-on and waiter at the door. Make your living any way you can, but neglect no sacrifice at your chosen altar. It may break your heart, it may drive you half mad, it may betray you into unrealizable ambitions or blind you to mercantile opportunities with its wandering fires. But it will fill your heart before it breaks it; it will make you a person in your own right; it will open the temple doors to you and enable you to walk with those who have come nearest among men to what men may sometime be.[2]

[2] From "Whatever Hope We Have" in *Essence of Tragedy* by Maxwell Anderson, copyright 1939. Used by permission of William Sloane Associates, Inc.

Alas! what boots it with uncessant care
To tend the homely, slighted Shepherds trade . . .
Were it not better done as others use,
To sport with Amaryllis in the shade,
Or with the tangles of Neaera's hair?
—MILTON, *Lycidas*

CHAPTER **9**

Library

Procedures

ALTHOUGH THIS is really a handbook for beginners in public library work with young people, it hardly seems necessary to go into a mass of procedural details. How do you mark your books to distinguish them from books in the adult collection? Are the books to be charged and discharged from the young people's corner or at the adult desk? What arrangement of shelving are you to use? Do you really want someone to tell you all these things? After all, your methods of procedure will depend entirely upon your own library, its size, the number on the staff, the amount of space allotted for young people's work, and the location of that space in relation to the adult department.

To my mind, there are two important principles of organization to be observed: young people's work should be tied in with the adult department rather than with the children's room, and all procedures should be made as simple as possible.

To insist upon the connection between the young people's setup and the adult department is in no way to disparage the excellence of the work done by the children's rooms or the relationships there established, but one of the deep-rooted desires of adolescence is for adult status, and that recognition can and should be accorded him. Your library will have to decide when he shall be given that recognition, at the attain

Little things

When is an adolescent an adult?

ment of a certain age or a certain grade, but do not delay it until you run the risk of losing him. The generally accepted time is at the beginning of the ninth grade, though many libraries give "Admit to Both Departments" cards a year earlier. The setting up of a young people's department should never limit him in his use of the library as a whole; both the children's room and the adult department should be hospitable to him; but the whole aim of this special work should be, as it is in the school library, to give him the equipment that will set him free in a world of books so that he may, with confidence and ease, turn to them all through his adult life.

As for simplifying procedures, this is simply a common sense recognition of the fact that too many regulations get in the way of library users, that routine work is never done any more than housework is, and that the librarian must decide what is of first importance in her work and question fiercely whatever distracts her from it. For too long a time, established routines have been supinely followed no matter what their cost, and quantities of records and statistics have been kept no matter what their value. Now that a dearth of personnel has necessitated a revaluation of duties, and the introduction of charging machines in many library systems has eliminated the possibility of keeping some customary records, it is a good time to question all library routines: do they facilitate or encumber the main business of the library which is *to bring together the reader and his essential book?*

Homing books   So look again at these introductory questions. How are you to mark these books so that, when they are returned, they will find their way back to the young people's corner? Not, I hope, by a special letter on the cover, although that plan commends itself to many busy libraries. Young people want assurance that their books are genuine adult books, and they have been accustomed to seeing a "J" marking children's books. They will be suspicious of any extra letter. Some libraries have a stamp, "Young People's Collection," on the inside cover of a book.

That will serve unless your shelves are stocked also by a good many books borrowed for a time from the adult department and eventually returned to its stock. In that case, a letter or a number or a symbol penciled somewhere on the inside cover where it will catch the eye of the librarian at the discharging desk will suffice and can be erased after the book has served its time in the special collection. The same notation may be penciled on the catalog card if this is the library's only copy of the book and if knowledge of its whereabouts is important.

Circulation   Are the books to be charged and discharged from your special section or at the main desk? In small libraries, at the main desk, of course. In large ones, there are good arguments for either procedure. If there is a special room for young people, it would certainly be easier to have all processes centered there. Is it a good idea, however, to keep your young folks from using regular adult channels? Do they need that protection? If so, it looks as if a little more understanding were needed on the part of other staff members. Some young people's rooms find the easiest solutions one of compromise: charge the books in the special room and have them returned at the main desk.

Shelving   As for shelving, there again it depends upon how large a collection you have. If it is small, keep it informal, arranged alphabetically by author or title. If it is sizeable, try subject arrangement, either Dewey or your own less detailed grouping. If it is large, there is much to be said for the ribbon arrangement—top shelf devoted to fiction, nonfiction below—since it scatters your readers of fiction around the room and betters the chances for nonfiction to catch the attention.

Finance   You know, by this time, the kind of books you want, and you have a pretty good idea of the number needed. How do you stretch your budget? Not by the purchase of cheap editions, though no book should be judged merely by its price-tag. Some reprints offer exceedingly good value and are attractive in format. For the most part, be skeptical of "movie" editions, and prefer "trade" to "school" editions. Of course the happiest solution would be for you to be able to see all these books before buying, but in many communities, that is still impossible. Should you be given a definite percentage of the book funds to spend for your collection? That seems only fair and businesslike. You may want to work out your own percentage, depending on number of borrowers in proportion to registered adults, or on circulation figures. Statistics in general would support a minimum figure of 25 per cent of the adult book funds. Your community may differ, and you may prefer to take a lower percentage and have the privilege of "indefinite loan" of desirable books from the adult department. If the head of the library is vigorously supporting the work, you will have funds and independence; if not, it may be wise for you to have a few figures at hand when you press your requests.

School libraries and cooperation   The size of your book collection will also be affected by the presence or lack of other book sources in your community, especially by the extent to which school libraries go in satisfying the book needs of their students. Relationship between high school library and public library should be one of generous cooperation, no matter what the form of organization. In some cities, the school libraries are staffed and administered by the public library; in others, the public library is also under the board of education; and in still others, there is no official connection but only an association of mutual respect and helpfulness, such as also exists between the public library and private and parochial schools. Each form of organization determines to some extent the services each institution renders to young people, but the most common assumption is that the school library shall provide material that implements the school curriculum and shall leave to the public library the opportunity of suggesting books for recreational reading. This sounds like a clear-cut division of responsibility, but even where the statement is true, its actual working out is far from simple. There is bound to be overlapping of functions and duplication of titles, for a book of information to one reader is recreational reading to another and vice versa, and as the school becomes increasingly community-centered rather than curriculum-centered, the books required by its students range far more widely than before.

Obviously, the school library is in a more advantageous position geographically for serving youth than is the public library. At least it is on the spot; it demands from its users no additional traveling, and this age of omnipresent communication aids discourages the zeal that spurred the young Lincoln to a twenty-mile jaunt for his book. The very fact that borrowers, young and old alike, approach the public library only when there is a "felt need" involves that institution in a program of publicity and makes it necessary for it to go out into the community and advise people who need it that it has what they need. Therein lies the main reason for your visits to schools and other outside agencies.

The free, voluntary reading that young people do in a public library makes it possible for us to uncover individual interests and reading capacities, a knowledge of which can be invaluable to school librarians and teachers alike. As a rule, the public library is freer to purchase and try out new books than is the school, is expected to have a wider range of materials, and can often suggest supplementary reading books which might supersede titles on established reading lists. Alertness in these matters on the part of the young people's librarian can be part of her contribution to a relationship that is mutually helpful and is an obligation she should be glad to assume. In return, she should be very sure that she understands the curriculum of the school, what the teachers are trying to accomplish, and how effective the school library is allowed to be.

What can you offer?

If the two institutions can work together in complete accord, they can accomplish much more for the young people concerned than if they pursue their ends independently, and, for that accord, there must be on both sides sympathetic understanding and a genuine desire for cooperation. This should not be difficult, since the goals are the same, and young people may be counted upon to understand any necessary differences in methods. That these differ far less than heretofore is demonstrated by the ease with which librarians go from one position to the other—from school library to public and vice versa.

As a representative of the public library, aware of the possibilities for joint action, you can approach the principal and the librarian of a school and offer them a program of such value that they will be willing to send classes to the public library for visits and informal talks, especially grades that are at the stage of transfer from the children's room to the adult department and again just before graduation. Now you can meet *all* the boys and girls, not only the ones who make a habit of using the public library. If the distance is too great to permit these visits, you may suggest your willingness to talk to classes in the school library or in the classrooms or in their homerooms, to explain what the public library has to offer and, in conjunction with the school, to suggest timely reading.

Every teacher knows how much it means to have an "outsider" emphasize to her students the very values she herself is seeking to inculcate. It not only brings a fresh point of view and unsolicited testimony, but it convinces some of the youthful skeptics that adults in real life situations find actual use for subjects now being explored in school and take delight in reading for pleasure authors now being studied. Here again the impression is made obliquely rather than directly.

A schedule of such visits may eventually be worked out through the librarian or the teacher of English or of the social studies. Talks in assemblies reach many more students than talks in classrooms but do not yield proportionate results. If they are suggested, don't ever avoid them unless you feel definitely unequal to them. There is no question as to the opportunity they offer and they provide excellent practice for you. They force you to make unusually careful preparation and to give thought to effectiveness of speech and manner that you might neglect in addressing smaller groups. And don't forget that you are not trying to attain forensic heights. You're there to extend an invitation to young people and to make the place you represent and the great cause you serve attractive to them.

As for reference work, no matter how excellent the facilities of the school library, there will be reference work enough for the two of you unless your schools have abolished "homework," and, if you understand the workings of the curriculum and are in touch with the current subject demands of the teachers, you can be prepared somewhat for the hordes of questioners who descend upon you. Where your reference work will be done is a matter dependent upon the setup of your library, but if it is not possible for you to handle it yourself, make sure that the reference assistant is also a person with understanding of youth and ability to interpret their requests. No school will thank you for doing the reference work *for* their students, but every growing boy and girl should be able to look confidently to public institutions for help when he needs it. *Reference work*

Some public libraries object to giving time and effort to help students with their school work, arguing that the school librarian should carry this responsibility. Much is to be gained, however, from this service. It brings young people into the public library. It affords an opportunity to help them find their way among books and to learn the use of library tools that will be valuable through adult life. It makes them feel that the public library is theirs to use for more purposes than recreational reading. It leads into individual research, as subjects of major interest to them grow and ramify. Not all reference help requested by young people is school work by any means, but draw the line on one and you will probably shut off the other as well.

You may be able to make some arrangement with the schools so that you will be notified automatically when a student drops out in order to go to work. Now you have another problem: how can you be sure of extending your service to him? Some libraries send postals or letters to these young people, reminding them of the vocational and technical and recreational books to *Out-of-school youth* be had, calling attention to evening hours of opening and to special programs planned for youth, and assuring them of their adult status.

Other groups   In approaching other youth-serving organizations, follow a similar plan. Know something of what they are doing and consider how the two of you, working together, can secure mutual benefit. Then lay such a plan before them. They in turn will have ideas and suggestions to offer, growing out of their special areas of service and their consciousness of the needs of young people. Together you should soon be able to formulate a workable program. If there is an over-all association of youth-serving organizations in your community, the public library should certainly be included, provided it has developed a definite service for young people. Through the Y.M.C.A., the Y.W.C.A., the Y.M.H.A. and others, you should be able to reach many out-of-school youth. When it comes to unions and employee groups of every kind, you will need to work through your own adult education department.

If your public library is already known as an active, invigorating force in the community, your work will be comparatively easy to develop and will soon fall into place in the entire program. If not, you will have the satisfaction that comes from pioneering and initiating such a program.

☞   . . . Nor do not saw the air too much with your hand, thus; but use all gently. . . . Be not too tame, neither, but let your own discretion be your tutor.

—SHAKESPEARE, *Hamlet*

Book Talks

LIBRARY WORK begins and ends with the individual. It welcomes group work but only as a way of reaching additional individuals. It responds to group requests but realizes that its response must be adapted to the varying capacities of the individual members. One of the most satisfactory means for reaching young people and interesting them in books is through the medium of book talks given before all kinds of groups.

It's always the individual

Foreknowledge of the group is desirable: age, sex, interests, current employment, intellectual attainment. The problem then becomes one of finding books that will reflect and hold their interest (and about which you yourself can be enthusiastic) and working out the best manner of presenting these books within strict time limits. They need not be new books, as Christopher Morley once pointed out. Writing in the *Saturday Review of Literature,* he had occasion to refer to his visit at the Crime Detection Laboratory at Northwestern University.

Book talks

There they have invented a way of reviving the most faded or perished ink-script. Unless the actual fabric of the paper has been destroyed, the ink leaves iron residues; and by blowing a gas upon an apparently blank sheet these particles of iron can be corroded so that the former writing leaps to sight, now rusted brilliant red. It struck me that here was a shiny parable for teachers of literature.

Their topic is often ancient books and papers, from which the childish pupil might suppose all life had withered. But if the teacher has the right kind of gas on spout, handwriting as old as Chaucer can burn again more vivid than tonight's tabloid. Presuming that it had, to begin with, the authentic mettle.

What books?   It is often wise to inject a few remarks about old favorites since it will add the reassurance of familiarity. They need not be primarily books of difficulty that need introduction. There is need for "bait" with a good many young people, and the approving mention of books that simply walk off from your shelves without even a friendly push from you will afford a quick revelation of your friendly and understanding attitude toward young people's reading.

Some librarians are tempted, looking at their shelves and seeing books that continue to stay there unread, simply to load up with an armful and go before a group to talk about them. That may be profitable, if you know your group very well, if you meet with them often, and if they have come to trust your judgment. But the opportunity that is afforded by book talks is not for the clearing of your shelves but the uncovering of individual interests and tastes and needs.

Begin   It is probably wise to start with the local, the immediate, the contemporary, to dispel at once any notion that a person working with books has no idea of what is happening in the world around him. Not only news and current happenings but radio programs and movies can supply you with opening sentences. From there move swiftly into the connecting book, by incident or character or conversation, and tell what you have come to tell with gusto and dispatch, savoring your recollection of the book as you go along and presenting it so that its special appeal, the thing that sets it apart from all other books, is apparent. Too many people, charmed by a fine piece of biographical writing, fall into the error, when facing a group and talking about it, of giving the bare facts of the subject's life and a summary of his accomplishments. They would be horri-

fied if you told them so, for the book is clear in their minds and
their remembrance of it pleases them even as they talk, but
they fail to convey any part of the book's charm. They might
have been reading an article in the encyclopedia for all their
auditors can make of it. The whole distinction of the book
is lost.

The book talk falls into place between storytelling and book
reviewing, partakes of both and is unlike either. At its best, it
sounds informal and spontaneous and in such harmony with
the group addressed that it seems like conversation or discussion
rather than a monologue. Back of this seeming spontaneity,
however, lie careful preparation and organization of material.

Think of the group you are to address, visualize them in your *Go on!*
mind's eye, place yourself among them, at one with them in
their occupations and surroundings, and cock an ear toward the
speaker who is just taking up his position in front of the group.
What do you want to hear? How do you wish to be addressed?
How long can you sit still and listen? Now, with that anticipa-
tion, consider your resources. You have the whole world of
books to choose from. Choose wisely, then, the book you will
present and refresh your recollection of it. Presumably you'd
like these young people to read it; then you must prove, simply
by your presentation, that it is worth reading. It will do no
good to say that it is exciting or thrilling: your youthful audience sits unmoved; obviously it is exciting or why would anyone
want to talk about it? They wait for evidence of the kind of
excitement they will find: the story must show it. Keep your
rendition of it moving along; don't let the narrative bog down
in details; don't clutter the listener's mind with too many characters to keep track of; keep your facts well in hand and well
reined in and drive on to a high moment, either of drama or
suspense. Leave it there, and, after enough of a pause to loose
your audience from the spell of the book, turn to another, one
that follows naturally, alike in some way or distinguished for
its utter dissimilarity.

*Watch
your group*

Watch your listeners as you talk—*all* of them—and see to it that you have something of interest for everyone, that before you finish, all of them will have heard something to remember. The friendliness of your manner, the sincerity of your approach, the understanding of your presentation, and the evidence of your respect for their opinion should make it easy for them to seek you out afterward and ask questions.

*Watch
yourself too!*

Naturally you'll make yourself heard by everyone and not confine your remarks to the first row or two, but you will capture their attention, not demand it. You might remember, too, that young people study Oral English and are quick to note carelessness in diction, sentence construction, posture, and all the rest. Is it necessary to add that of course you will not use notes and that the books you talk about will be in your hands as you speak and available from your library later on?

If you are talking about novels or biography, make the characters live as they live on the pages. Let them walk out of the books and into the lives of your listeners. Sketch them vividly in a few words so that they are recognizable, and give concrete examples of their actions, not some abstract generalizations as to their line of conduct. Even though your zeal to make your auditors want to read the book for themselves tempts you to over-ornamentation, avoid it sternly. Better lose readers than have readers disappointed through your excess of enthusiasm.

*Go on
talking*

Sometimes your desire to "be faithful to the book" will persuade you that reading aloud from it will be far more effective than relating the story in your own words. "The author can say it much better." Very likely, else you yourself would be an author, but right now it is your job to talk. You have established a rapport with your group; they are giving you their attention and enjoying it; things are moving along rapidly and well. Don't jeopardize that relationship; go on telling in your own words (heightened perhaps by phrases remembered from the author's own recital) and to the very best of your ability "what happened next."

The only legitimate time for you to read to a group is when *This is*
you are presenting material in which the author's style is the *parenthetical*
important thing and can be communicated in no other way:
poetry, some essays, fine writing in general. Even then you
would do well to quote rather than to read or know the book
so well that you are not bound to it—your eyes can still rove
over the group and take cognizance of their enjoyment, be
watchful for signs of disinterest.

If you are presenting factual material or technical books, be
very sure of your terms and be able to bandy them about
masterfully. Sharpen your descriptions. Strive always for the
concrete instance, the definite fact.

And throw in something definitely beyond their expectations *Here's*
even if it occasionally goes over their heads. Sometimes a casual *your chance*
phrase, an interpolated reference to advanced material may be
the one thing to catch a reader's attention and start him off on a
quest of his own. Pay them the compliment of assuming that
they are willing and eager to stretch their minds even when all
evidence would seem to point to the contrary.

Know beforehand what your allotment of time is to be and *Here's*
keep well within it. Plan your talk thoroughly in a kind of *your hat—*
outline or within a frame, force yourself to practice it aloud
with your watch in your hand and cut drastically where necessary. If you retain too much or are unwilling to plan and,
therefore, improvise and expand as you go along, you will find
yourself hurrying your speech and talking briskly with no room
for the little play of stress and drawl and pause that can be so
effective and that make for informality. Your listeners are not
going to be at ease unless you are at ease; so be sure of your
material. Otherwise you may find yourself looking at your
watch and commenting on the shabbily few minutes you have,
thus transferring everyone's attention from the matter at hand
to an anxiety lest you fail to stop in time. Be sure you do *that*—
stop in time—before interest wanes. You may be asked to
come again.

As one who, reading in a book some word
That calls joy back, but can recall not where—
Only a crazy sweetness in the head—
Will stare at the black print till the page is blurred.
                                        —MacLeish, *Pony Rock*

CHAPTER **11**

Book Association

ONE OF THE most valuable assets you can have in your work with young people, and one that will stand you in good stead in floor work and in book talks, is your ability to associate books in various ways. Of course, the most natural way is by author and subject. If a boy has read *Treasure Island* and wants another book, we reach for *Kidnapped*. If he returns *Smoky* and looks expectant, we recommend *My Friend Flicka* or *King of the Stallions*. This is good as far as it goes, and we would do well to know the subject matter of books thoroughly so as to relate them in this way.

But there are various meanings in books, and the better we know them at firsthand, the easier it will be for us to exchange comments with young people and recommend books that will go a little farther afield. Let's say a boy returns *Lassie-Come-Home*, likes it and wants another book "just like it." Must it be a dog story? If so, there are plenty of choices, including books on the sheep dog trials and the seeing-eye dogs. But could it be the relationship between a boy and his pet that has impressed the reader? Then *My Friend Flicka* and *The Yearling* come to mind, perhaps *Herdboy of Hungary*. Might it be the family understanding that meant something to him? If so, there are scores of titles. Did he enjoy the setting, the

"That reminds me"

English and Scottish countryside? Capitalize on that while you can.

One way
to get
wide reading

Suppose a girl returns *Mama's Bank Account*, which she has thoroughly enjoyed. Where can you go from there? It would certainly seem to be the character of Mama that makes the impression. How about the mother in Saroyan's *Human Comedy*? Or *Happy Mountain*? How about going back to *Mrs. Wiggs*? Or to Eliza in *The Friendly Persuasion*? Or to Selina in *So Big*? Is it, perhaps, the foreigner in America, experiencing some difficulty with our ways? Try *Anything Can Happen* or *My American Adventure*—and don't forget Bojer's *The Emigrants*. Does Norway seem a little nearer? There's *Northern Summer* and *Norwegian Farm* and *Happy Times in Norway*—and *Beyond Sing the Woods* and *Kristin Lavransdatter*.

Of whom will Alice Adams remind you? In her pathetic desire to appear at advantage, isn't she very like the old lady herself in *The Old Lady Shows Her Medals*? And when you read of Henriette in *All This and Heaven Too* or of the young wife in *Rebecca*, don't you remember *Jane Eyre*? Don't you associate Rhett Butler with Gaylord Ravenal and with the young adventurer of *Frenchman's Creek*? Aren't there similarities between the old lady in *The House of the Seven Gables* and those in *Cranford*? Could Mrs. Lecks and Mrs. Aleshine join the company, or Tish or Betsey Trotwood? And doesn't Micawber, when he isn't resembling W. C. Fields, resemble Toad?

Any book may be, and actually is, a starting point for your whole library collection. And these associations unfold, not in any conscious "ladder" arrangement, but more as spokes in a wheel.

To the haphazard reader who somehow expects to read everything before he gets through, aimless as he may seem, it is fun to play with titles: *Immortal Wife*; *My Chinese Wife*; *Wilderness Wife*; *Cowman's Wife*; *The Man Who Married a Dumb Wife*; or *The Wind and the Rain*; *Who Has Seen the Wind*;

*Wind, Sand and Stars; Wind in the Willows; Windswept;
East Wind, West Wind; Fresh Wind Blowing; Gone with
the Wind; Let the Hurricane Roar!*

When you are letting books group themselves together in
your mind as you plan a talk, never think you must be limited
to a subject, though that is one way of going about it: books
on the Middle Ages, books of exploration (this might include
almost every endeavor), new books, books that have won prizes,
etc. This is sometimes a necessary concession to make to
groups, but if you are free in your choice, let your mind range—
within the bounds, of course, of your audience's interests.

Book talks

Perhaps you've been telling the story, *The Ransom of Red
Chief*. Do you know any other boys whom kidnappers might
gladly pay to be rid of? Your group will joyfully help you out,
especially if they have small brothers: *Little Orvie, There's
One in Every Family, Tom Sawyer, Aram, Tree Toad*. Or
perhaps you've introduced *Jamba the Elephant*. Give a thought
to a few of his predecessors: Alice in *Lions'n'Tigers'n'Everything*, the sweet-potato-loving elephant in *Safari*, the Elephant's
Child in the *Just So Stories*, Bunner's *Zenobia* . . . .

These are just by-the-way suggestions. You will think of
countless others. Casual references may be made in this way
without delaying your talk too much.

Sometimes you link one book to another by a comment, a
descriptive phrase. You may have been talking, let us say,
about *Jamaica Inn*, and, having conveyed a strong sense of that
foreboding atmosphere, you end by saying, "*Anything* could
happen in a house like that!" Does that phrase suggest other
houses? Of course it does. Let your audience join in: *The Old
Dark House, Wuthering Heights, The Uninvited, Rebecca, Fall
of the House of Usher*. "She was a young lady with a will of
her own"; "He suddenly felt all alone in the world"; "Greater
love hath no man than this"; "Curiouser and curiouser"—set
up a few phrases like these and watch the books cluster
around them.

A good exercise in book association is to take a short list of books familiar to you and for each book set down a few other titles that may be linked with it either through character (even minor characters), incident, or setting. It will impress upon you the necessity for reading widely and for making mental notes, or perhaps written ones, as you read. It will also make even more evident the fact that, though books are reminiscent of one another, they are also individual and stand alone, true to themselves. "Give you a book like *Mama's Bank Account?* My dear girl, there just isn't any book like it. Bring me a girl just like yourself, and then I'll find you a book just like *Mama's Bank Account.*" (But be sure you're not talking to one of a pair of identical twins.)

Floor work   There are two questions you must be prepared to meet over and over again in floor work, one of which has already been stated: "Have you got another book like this one?" The other is asked by the person who picks up a book, thumbs through it hastily, and turns to you with the expectancy that is the greatest compliment he can pay you, "Is this a good book? Will I like it? What's it about?" Innocent sounding question, but it calls for all your training, your firsthand knowledge of the book and your ability to size up the inquirer quickly. You believe in the high-sounding "reading guidance." You aspire to practice it. All right, now's the time! You didn't really think it meant you could settle down with a teen ager and leisurely discuss his life problems and plan a well-integrated course of reading for him, did you? But these priceless opportunities for quick discussion, rapid-fire summaries of books, their salient points, their relevance, and recommendation will come again and again if you measure up to them. So give a little thought to thumb-nail descriptions—not reviews—of books and learn to get the telling things, the points of special interest to young people, said quickly.

With the noninquirer, the young person who never directly approaches you for aid though he sometimes seems to be pretty helpless, you must develop a different technique. Learn to recognize the independent, exploring type of reader and respect his independence. Do the same with those who are really not readers but just enjoy a quiet sojourn by the shelves and *don't want to be talked to*. Don't hound any possible reader out of the library by the assiduity of your attentions. But if you should just happen near the shelves by which they are standing, you can often draw their attention to a book without seeming to, simply by taking it down from the shelf, looking through it and replacing it, so easily is one's attention distracted. Rely on the appeal of the book, its appearance, its place on the shelf (don't ever crowd your shelves: leave room for books to breathe and stir around and present more than their spines to the reader), and its very proximity.

Once the young people become accustomed to having you around, not chattering at them but astonishingly able to give answers when questioned and talk over with them the inner workings of books, you will have your hands full of possibilities for reading guidance.

STEVENSON, ROBERT L. Treasure Island. Scribner
——— Kidnapped. Scribner
JAMES, WILL. Smoky. Scribner
O'HARA, MARY. My Friend Flicka. Lippincott.
TRACY, EDWARD B. King of the Stallions. Dodd, Mead

KNIGHT, ERIC. Lassie-Come-Home. Winston
RAWLINGS, MARJORIE. The Yearling. Scribner
FINTA, ALEXANDER. Herdboy of Hungary. Harper

FORBES, KATHRYN. Mama's Bank Account. Harcourt, Brace
SAROYAN, WILLIAM. The Human Comedy. Harcourt, Brace
CHAPMAN, MARISTAN. The Happy Mountain. Viking
RICE, ALICE HEGAN. Mrs. Wiggs of the Cabbage Patch. Appleton-Century
WEST, JESSAMYN. The Friendly Persuasion. Harcourt, Brace
FERBER, EDNA. So Big. Grosset

Books mentioned in this chapter

PAPISHVILY, GEORGE. Anything Can Happen. Harper
BARSCHAK, ERNA. My American Adventure. Ives Washburn
BOJER, JOHAN. The Emigrants. Appleton-Century
GEIJERSTAM, GUSTAV. Northern Summer. Dutton
UNDSET, SIGRID. Happy Times in Norway. Knopf
GULBRANSSEN, TRYGVE. Beyond Sing the Woods. Putnam
UNDSET, SIGRID. Kristin Lavransdatter. Knopf

TARKINGTON, BOOTH. Alice Adams. Grosset
BARRIE, JAMES M. The Old Lady Shows Her Medals (in *Plays*).
  Scribner
FIELD, RACHEL. All This and Heaven Too. Macmillan
DU MAURIER, DAPHNE. Rebecca. Doubleday
BRONTË, CHARLOTTE. Jane Eyre. World
MITCHELL, MARGARET. Gone with the Wind. Macmillan
FERBER, EDNA. Show Boat. Grosset
DU MAURIER, DAPHNE. Frenchman's Creek. Garden City
HAWTHORNE, NATHANIEL. The House of the Seven Gables. Hough-
  ton, Mifflin
GASKELL, ELIZABETH. Cranford. Bell
STOCKTON, FRANK. The Casting Away of Mrs. Lecks and Mrs.
  Aleshine. Appleton-Century
RINEHART, MARY ROBERTS. More Tish. Triangle
DICKENS, CHARLES. David Copperfield. Macrae Smith
GRAHAME, KENNETH. The Wind in the Willows. Scribner

STONE, IRVING. Immortal Wife. Doubleday
ESKELUND, KARL. My Chinese Wife. Grosset
PINKERTON, KATHRENE. Wilderness Wife. Grosset
RAK, MARY K. Cowman's Wife. Houghton, Mifflin
FRANCE, ANATOLE. The Man Who Married a Dumb Wife. Dodd,
  Mead

HORNER, JOYCE. The Wind and the Rain. Doubleday
MITCHELL, WILLIAM. Who Has Seen the Wind? Little, Brown
SAINT-EXUPÉRY, ANTOINE DE. Wind, Sand and Stars. Reynal
CHASE, MARY ELLEN. Windswept. Macmillan
BUCK, PEARL. East Wind, West Wind. John Day
CAMPBELL, GRACE. Fresh Wind Blowing. Duell
LANE, ROSE WILDER. Let the Hurricane Roar. Longmans

PORTER, SYDNEY. The Ransom of Red Chief (short story)
TARKINGTON, BOOTH. Little Orvie. Doubleday
EISENBERG, FRANCES. There's One in Every Family. Lippincott
CLEMENS, SAMUEL L. The Adventures of Tom Sawyer. Harper
SAROYAN, WILLIAM. My Name is Aram. Harcourt, Brace
DAVIS, BOB. Tree Toad. Lippincott

WALDECK, THEODORE. Jamba the Elephant. Viking
COOPER, COURTNEY R. Lions'n'Tigers'n'Everything. Little, Brown
JOHNSON, MARTIN. Safari. Putnam
KIPLING, RUDYARD. Just So Stories. Doubleday
BUNNER, HENRY. Zenobia's Infidelity (short story)

DU MAURIER, DAPHNE. Jamaica Inn. Pocket Books
PRIESTLEY, J. B. The Old Dark House. New American Lib.
BRONTË, EMILY. Wuthering Heights. Dutton
MACARDLE, DOROTHY. The Uninvited. Doubleday
POE, EDGAR A. The Fall of the House of Usher (short story)

I must read Whitman again, and Keats again.
I overheard somebody saying the name,
Someone excited, thinking about these men . . .
                    —JOHN HOLMES, *After Two Years*

CHAPTER 12

Book
Reminders

MODERN DEVELOPMENTS in the techniques of communication have been startlingly effective and can be yours to conjure with. "Audio-visual" is the deplorable but descriptive term under which most of these aids cluster. If some librarians have been slow to see their potentialities, it is a good thing for the human race that not all people who deal with ideas have been so blind to their significance, that we can thank them for the "talking book," the projected book, the voices of poets reading their own verses, of actors interpreting dramatic passages, of states-men immortalizing their own day. To belabor the movies and the radio for cheap programs and ill effects and to disregard the fine contributions they have made is to throw out the baby with the bath. To young people born into a world where these aids are everyday matters, it is unthinkable that books should be divorced from film, phonograph, and radio. All are avenues of communication and can usefully complement one another. It is the testimony of librarians that the presentation of a story in the movies or its dramatization on the radio, far from injuring the circulation of the book involved, actually increases it.

Audio-visual aids

Many libraries have formed listening groups for radio pro-grams with discussion following the broadcast. Young people are invariably attracted to such meetings and usually add to the

Listening groups

significance and the sociability of forums. A sprinkling of them in adult groups is beneficial to both sides, but if it is evident that a large section of your youthful population is interested, they should be granted forums of their own. If you initiate such programs in your library, be sure you have an alert, objective, and highly capable leader. Don't think you must do all these things yourself. You doubtless have some limitations— of time if not ability. You may even be too close to the group to preside dispassionately over their discussions.

Film forums   There are also such things as "film forums" which can be exceedingly effective but are not casually to be undertaken. Select your film with the same care you exercise in selecting books. See it, if possible, before booking it. Aim your advance publicity at the age group you consider best fitted to discuss it and ruthlessly exclude from the showing, perhaps by requiring tickets, those distracting elements who might throng the place out of sheer curiosity to "see the pictures." Start your discussion period immediately after the showing of the film, by throwing out some provocative question or statement, and carry it along while the interest is sustained. Never hesitate to conclude earlier than expected rather than flog and belabor the discussion.

Music   Evenings of music are welcomed by young people—radio, *programs*   phonograph, or "live musicians." Such programs may be more informal than the film forums and can be arranged and conducted by the young people themselves. Let them choose their favorite selections. You will often be surprised at the sureness with which they move about in this territory and by the richness of their musical knowledge and appreciation, so completely has symphonic and orchestral music penetrated to them through the radio and the phonograph. As for jazz, it is their natural idiom and they explore its intricacies with delight.

Book   With all these lively and entertaining affairs, you will not *displays*   forget to associate books. They have a rightful place and need never look ill at ease in any of these gatherings. Sometimes they will enter into the discussions, as references are made to them and perhaps questions settled by their use. Sometimes— usually, in fact—they will be in evidence because of special displays you have arranged for the occasion. If poster-making is not your forte, there's probably some gifted youngster around who would be glad to help you out. But posters are not always necessary; special groupings of the books themselves in attractive jackets, if possible, on a table near the entrance or at the back of the room, will call attention to themselves better than any other device.

If you can have mimeographed or printed lists to hand out after the discussions, you should certainly learn how to write provocative annotations. Try to get away altogether from the critical or evaluative note your fellow-librarian would want if she were considering purchase of the book; keep your youthful reader very distinctly in mind and aim a shaft at him that will bring him down in search of the book. Avoid questions and exclamation marks; they give a sense of "talking down." Be explanatory or descriptive and yet reticent—never effusive. A good annotation of this kind is really a book talk *in parvo.* It has the same innocent air of appearing to satisfy curiosity while it increases it. I have always liked this one on Saint-Exupéry's *Night Flight,* written by one of my students at Columbia:

Book notes

> Rivière, Superintendent of the Air Mail, had a motto. It was: if you punish men enough, the weather will improve. But this time, the weather didn't improve.

Once you acquire the knack of dashing off succinct and teasing annotations, you will find countless opportunities to use them—your bulletin board, the school paper, perhaps your local paper. Let the young people try their hand at it also and encourage them to write their comments on books they have read to guide their fellows who are searching for the right book. Accept short notes, even adjectives, or long reviews, but empha size the fact that they will be without value unless they express the genuine and considered opinion of the writer.

Book questions   The popularity of quiz shows on the radio makes it possible now to ask questions of young people without any of the fearsome aspects of examinations. They enter heartily into all such programs and enjoy adding features that copy or burlesque radio. Questions of this kind should, like annotations, be neat and flavorsome: not "When did Dickens write *Tale of Two Cities?*" or even "Who wrote *Tale of Two Cities?*" but "Who spent his time in prison making shoes?", a question that should beguile the answerer into a recollection of the book so vivid that he may find himself suddenly talking about it. Don't try to describe the book by questions, lead into it; you can have a chance for a two-minute book talk almost any time. "Who calmly continued the Latin lesson during an air raid?" "Who broke the great pancake record?" "What was the name of Mr. Mifflin's traveling bookshelf?" Include questions on books that you know will be familiar so as to put your group at ease; include others that will almost inevitably lead to short book talks and discussions. Try anything that will get boys and girls talking about books and enjoying it—games in which authors and titles are matched in old-fashioned "spelling down" style, and others. You will think of scores of games that can be adapted for your purpose if evenings like this are possible in your library.

But after all, these are "extra-curricular activities" calculated to attract attention and inspire good feeling. Your core curriculum is still the individual and his book. Let nothing divert you from that.

Epilogue

ARE YOU feeling a bit staggered by all the possibilities outlined for you? Does it seem as if everything depended on you, that you are the one responsible for book talks and individual discussions and reading guidance, and that whether or not the young people in your community grow up with a taste for reading depends on how you measure up to your job? That's only partly true. There's enough truth in it to keep you everlastingly working to fit yourself for your chosen occupation, but neither the responsibility nor the actual endeavor is yours alone. The school librarian feels exactly the same. So does the English teacher. So do parents. Every decent element in the community is working right along with you. *It's a big job!*

You are not alone

And so, while never losing sight of the importance of your work, don't overvalue it either. Lend yourself to the life around you. Neither schooling nor education comes entirely through books. Books deal with ideas, it is true, sometimes with great ideas. They enlarge a community, so that men of all countries and of ages past and gone can still be actively at work advising and conversing with those who face the problems of today and have to act upon them. But it would be a dismal prospect if the makers of today's world had nothing to add to what has been said before. Be alive to the accents of your own day and your own neighbors and vigilant to recognize their worth and importance. Occasionally try out your own voice, too. In other words, be a good participating citizen, not "just a librarian." Professionalism should provide you with additional and valuable resources, not protective coloration.

If the foregoing chapters have not yet conveyed to you the challenge and the rewards of this work, the refreshing and invigorating currents that flow constantly back from aroused youth, and the sheer delight to be found in the materials at your command, then I cannot hope to accomplish it in this brief afterword. It is not only the heartfelt but embarrassed growl of thanks that occasionally escapes the inarticulate boy, or the increased confidence with which the young people, under your surreptitious guidance, find their homeward way among books. These are gratifying signs, to be sure, but they

The "why" of it all

are only signs. The real satisfactions go deeper. They lie in our awareness that we are part of the great concourse of workers who are moved by a profound belief in three important factors: *the power of the book* to inject ideas, to stir the reader to thought and action, and to demonstrate anew the blessed relief of communication to the ineluctable loneliness of man; *the power of the individual* to dominate his material and so to free himself to develop, in his own best way, the innate capacities of his nature; and *the power of democracy* to seek its highest expression in the free circulation of ideas and the greatest possible liberation of individual endowments.

That we share these beliefs and, even in these troubled times, are privileged to act upon them in such ways as to testify daily to our faith should be an energizing impulse to quicken our zeal.

But all these things are not for telling now;
I have, God knows, an ample field to plow. . . .

Index

Questions, use of, 114
Quiller-Couch. *Oxford Book of English Verse*, 74, 77

Raine. *Sheriff's Son*, 35, 42
Rak. *Cowman's Wife*, 104, 108
Rama Rau. *Home to India*, 52, 54
Raspe. *Surprising Adventures of Baron Munchausen*, 31, 40
Rawlings. *Yearling*, 51, 53, 103, 107
Readability, 83
Reade. *Cloister and the Hearth*, 46, 53
Reading, condemnation of, 24, 48; motivation for, 13-15, 17, 65, 69, 74, 76
Reading aloud, 15, 50, 100
Reading difficulties, 67-68
Reading guidance, 23-24, 37, 46, 61
Reading interests, 9-10, 30, 45
Reading of young people's librarian, 10, 16, 22, 29-30, 49, 51, 74, 83-84, 106
Reading promotion, 25, 111ff.
Reese, quoted, 38
Reference books, 82, 93
Repplier. *In Our Convent Days*, 51, 54
Retarded readers, 9, 36, 58, 67-68, 69, 81, 82-83, 98
Rhodes. *Proud Sheriff*, 35, 42
Ribbon arrangement, 89
Rice. *Mrs. Wiggs of the Cabbage Patch*, 104, 107
Rinehart. *Circular Staircase*, 35, 41. *More Tish*, 104, 108
Rizk. *Syrian Yankee*, 51, 53
Roberts. *Rabble in Arms*, 46, 53
Robinson, E. A. *Tristram*, 46, 52
Robinson, J. *My Own Story*, 31, 40
Romance, 45ff.
Roos. *Man of Molokai*, 42
Ross. *Education of H*Y*M*A*N* K*A*P*L*A*N**, 70, 77
Rostand. *Cyrano de Bergerac*, 46, 52
Rourke. *Davy Crockett*, 36, 42
Ryerson. *This Awful Age*, 3-4, 11

Sabatini. *Captain Blood*, 38, 42
Saint-Exupéry. *Night Flight*, 34, 41; *Wind, Sand, and Stars*, 105, 108
Sandburg. *The People, Yes*, 51, 54; quoted, 51, 56
Saroyan. *Human Comedy*, 104, 107; *My Name Is Aram*, 105, 109
Sayers. *Strong Poison*, 41
School libraries, 22, 90-93
School stories, 32
School visiting, 92
Science, 59-60
Science fiction, 33
Scoggin. *Lure of Danger*, 39, 42
Scott. *Talisman*, 46, 53
Sea stories, 37-38
Sex education, 59
Shakespeare. *Romeo and Juliet*, 46, 52; quoted, 96
Shapiro. *John Magarac and His U.S.A. Citizen Papers*, 33, 41; *John Henry and the Double-Jointed Steam-Drill*, 33, 41
Shepard. *Paul Bunyan*, 33, 40
Short stories, 69
Shute. *No Highway*, 34, 41
Skariatina. *World Can End*, 52, 54
Spence. *One Foot in Heaven*, 51, 53
Sperry. *Lost Lagoon*, 69, 76
Sports, 31
Staff, attitude toward young people, 21, 89, 93
Stephens. *Crock of Gold*, 46, 52
Stevenson. *Kidnapped*, 42, 103, 107; *Treasure Island*, 42, 103, 107; quoted, 72
Stockton. *Casting Away of Mrs. Lecks and Mrs. Aleshine*, 104, 108
Stone. *Immortal Wife*, 104, 108
Stout. *And Be a Villain*, 41
Strain. *Teen Days*, 59, 62

Tall tales, 33
Tarkington. *Alice Adams*, 51, 53, 104, 108; *Little Orvie*, 105, 109; *Seventeen*, 3, 11, 70, 76
Teale. *Dune Boy*, 51, 53
Technical books, 57ff.
Tennyson, quoted, 51